GW01417426

PLANET GAUGE

by

Rowland Morgan

FOURTH ESTATE · *London*

First published in Great Britain in 1992 by
Fourth Estate Limited
289 Westbourne Grove
London W11 2QA

Copyright © Rowland Morgan 1992

The right of Rowland Morgan to be identified as the author of
this work has been asserted by him in accordance with the
Copyright, Designs and Patents Act 1988.

A catalogue record for this book is available from the British
Library

ISBN 1–85702–087–1

All rights reserved. No part of this publication may be
reproduced, transmitted or stored in a retrieval system,
in any form or by any means, without permission in writing
from Fourth Estate Limited.

Typeset by York House Typographic Ltd, London
Printed in Great Britain by Cox and Wyman Ltd, Reading,
Berks.

Acknowledgements: To Lewis Lapham and *Harpers Index* of Hudson Valley Bioregion, Turtle Island, for starting a trend; Ian Jack and the *Independent on Sunday*, Thames Valley Bioregion, England, for following it up; the staff at the excellent new on-line Public Library of the City of Miami, River of Grass Bioregion, Turtle Island; the staff at the Reference Library of Richmond Upon Thames; Giles O'Bryen of Fourth Estate publishers; Edward Goldsmith; O. M. Lewis; Jane Taylor; Janet Alty; Ian Henshall; and to the writers and editors of all the parliamentary services, reports, newsletters, journals, almanacs, polemics, poems, etc., from which this information sprang. Any errors in this compilation of it are the editor's.

READOUT ARRAY

Navigator's Report
UK Zone   1–517
First Class Zone   518–722
Southern Hemisphere Zone   723–817
Command Centre   818–925
Human Factors   926–1016
Resource Control   1017–1110
Supply Hold   1111–1220
On-board Energy Systems   1221–1313
Climate Control   1314–1415
Waste Management   1416–1505
Sources & Notes

▶ ▶NAVIGATOR'S REPORT

Spaceship Earth, Solar System, The Universe
Submitted to Command Deck AD 1993 from Control Room

GAUGE DECK REPORT

Nothing focuses thought like a well-chosen numerical fact. Numbers are hard, they have clarity, they sock home a point. Few words can sum up Africa's problems as immediately as readout *731*. Readout *402* says it all about the eco-blindness of contemporary Britain. And *580* emphasises how every book should be weighed for its worth against the trees it fells before it goes to press.

There's a huge scope of info-power packed into these pages, with 1,505 nuggets gleaned from hundreds of primary sources for pondering, playing with, or passing on. In addition, each individual readout is the key to thousands of strings of further figures set up by a web of cross-references.

If you can't believe some of the stunners listed, check the sources. There are hundreds of extra details in the notes. We hope by assembling this rack of readings we saved you busy Earthlings some paper, and some time – you sure need it!

Plenty of the world's facts are hard to face; but there's no denying it, this is the only world we've got. As Space Bardics Officer Wendell Berry says, we have to 'look the facts in the face and smile'.

Rowland Morgan
Control Room, Gauge Deck
Earth

[1] **£30,319,000** Spend of UK advertisers each working day ▷▷ *445*

[2] **£83,077,000** Spend on UK education each working day ▷▷ *223*   ▷▷ *445*

[3] **55** Wembley Stadiums of people looking after an elderly or dependent relative ▷▷ *338*

[4] **42,000,000** Acres being farmed in Great Britain ▷▷ *185* ▷▷ *1058*

[5] **34,593** Acres being farmed organically ▷▷ *64* ▷▷ *853*

[6] **2** Number of times British derelict hedgerows would circle the globe ▷▷ *171*   ▷▷ *234*   ▷▷ *400*

[7] **£17,500,000** Annual budget for paying British farmers not to farm ▷▷ *171*

[8] **£2,000,000,000** Taxes spent subsidising agriculture annually ▷▷ *706*

[9] **£17,180,000,000** Government support for UK agriculture, forestry and fishing in next decade at current rate ▷▷ *1079*

[10] **£18,000,000,000** Fiat's planned top spend on new car models in next decade ▷▷ *1413, 1414*

[11] **1,334** Juggernaut loads of pesticide-active ingredients sold per year ▷▷ *873*

[12] **3** Number of times road tankers loaded with a year's road traffic emissions of deadly carbon monoxide would stretch nose-to-tail from Glasgow to Brighton ▷▷ *1413, 1414*

[13] **£31,000** Average working day's expenditure planned by the Department of the Environment for monitoring air quality ▷▷ *14*   ▷▷ *286*

[14] **£31,538** Average working day's expenditure planned by the Department of the Environment on government ministers' limousine service ▷▷*856*

[15] **£56,538** Average working day's expenditure planned by the Department of the Environment on government security guards in London ▷▷*114, 115*

[16] **10,000,000** Aluminium cans littered or dumped every day ▷▷*355*　▷▷*707*　▷▷*1416*

[17] **489** White-fronted Amazon parrots imported in 1988 ▷▷*536*　▷▷*1368*

[18] **822** Abattoir owners in the UK ▷▷*665* ▷▷*1394*

[19] **2.2** Chickens per Briton ▷▷*21*　▷▷*769, 770* ▷▷*1210*

[20] **4,340,688** Number of cows in the UK ▷▷*183*　▷▷*1017*

[21] **10,376,354** Live poultry shipped to Europe per year ▷▷*571*

[22] **753** Miles of nose-to-tail juggernaut loads of dead animal waste processed by renderers each year ▷▷*1072, 1073*

[23] **75,681** British sheep slaughtered on average working day ▷▷*724, 725*

[24] **11,000,000** Turkeys slaughtered for Christmas each year ▷▷*571*

[25] **11,000** Dogs used for laboratory experiments per year ▷▷*358, 359*

[26] **206,000** Lethal whole-body toxicity tests on live animals per year ▷▷*34*

[27] **200** Heron shot per year by Scottish salmon farmers

[28] **50,000** Deer cull required in the Highlands of Scotland each year ▷▷*571*

[29] **42** Juggernaut loads of faeces deposited by British dogs per day ▷▷*479*

[30] **£191,000** Annual upkeep cost of H M Queen's horses and carriages ▷▷*366*

[31] **31,163,000** Sheep and lambs in UK in 1979 ▷▷*570*

[32] **44,217,000** Sheep and lambs in UK today ▷▷*568* ▷▷*572*

[33] **1,000,000** Animals killed on roads each year ▷▷*685*

[34] **17,000,000** Antibiotic shots sent up the teats of UK dairy cows each year ▷▷*618*

[35] **£2,251** UK assets of USA banks per UK resident ▷▷*804*

[36] **£4,097** UK assets of Japanese banks per UK resident ▷▷*823*

[37] **2,240,000** Tonnes of coal-equivalent energy used annually by 35m increase in Bangladesh's population expected by year 2000 ▷▷ *795, 796*

[38] **20,000,000** Tonnes of coal-equivalent energy used annually by 4m increase in UK's population since 1961 ▷▷*278*

[39] **£1,734** Annual taxpayer support paid to London Borough of Hackney per capita ▷▷ *775*

[40] **£535** Annual taxpayer support paid to Newcastle-upon-Tyne per capita

[41] **2** Percentage of people proud of Britain's economic achievements ▷▷ *141, 142*

[42] **£454** UK residents' annual earnings from overseas investments per capita ▷▷ *759*

[43] **£89** Third World debt to each Briton through government credits ▷▷ *781*

[44] **20,000,000** Packages of disposable babywipes sold each year ▷▷ *895*

[45] **20,000** Hours chemicals in throwaway-nappy fibre rub against a baby's flesh ▷▷ *618*

[46] **2,877,000,000** Throwaway nappies disposed of each year by UK parents ▷▷ *711*   ▷▷ *810*

[47] **99** Percentage of US mothers' milk containing significant levels of pesticide DDT ▷▷ *618*

[48] **2** Farms near Bolsover where dioxin poisons have been found in cows' milk ▷▷ *421*   ▷▷ *618*

[49] **£220,000** Taxpayer support for MPs on an average working day ◁◁ *14*

[50] **$17,010,000,000** Total foreign debt of Pakistan (population: 105m) ▷▷ *760*

[51] **$19,400,000,000** Total reported debt of Olympia & York, developer of London's Canary Wharf, before bankruptcy ◁◁ *50*

[52] **2,535,148** Home visits made by social workers to discuss benefits in 1985 ▷▷ *239, 240*

[53] **870,642** Home visits made by social workers to discuss benefits in 1989 ▷▷ *374, 375*

[54] **£5** Cost of administering each weekly £36.95 income-support payment for person over 25 ▷▷ *491, 492*

[55] **1.5** Days' reduction in processing each Income Support Claim achieved by £1.2bn automation

[56] **£33,000,000** Cost per hour of delay saved by automation

[57] **0.5** Estimated grams of carcinogenic petrochemicals ingested each day by a typical Briton ▷▷ *70* ▷▷ *1325*

[58] **25,888** Cyclists killed or injured on public roads per year ▷▷ *365* ▷▷ *1325*

[59] **£279,500,000** Fees paid to City brokers for privatisations by the DTI ▷▷ *549*

[60] **£2,500,000** Aid to Bangladeshi cyclone victims

[61] **20** Bosses under age 45 whose total reported income in 1991 was over £500,000 ▷▷ *171*

[62] **219** Miles juggernauts would stretch loaded nose-to-tail with a year's production of polypropylene plastics ▷▷ *187*

[63] **20** Percentage of domestically produced bottles that are made from recycled glass ▷▷ *1434*

[64] **22** Percentage of 148 UK bread samples found to contain residues of pesticides Clorpyrifos-methyl, Etrimphos, Lindane, Malathion and Pirimphos-methyl ▷▷ *1080*

[65] **£84,600,000** Fast-breeder reactor research budget for 1991–2 of the Department of Energy ▷▷ *893*

[66] **£11,000,000** Energy efficiency research budget for 1991–2 of the Department of Energy ▷▷ *350*

[67] **172** Juggernaut loads of surplus butter given away in 1990 ▷▷ *706*

[68] **11,000,000** Households with cable TV in West Germany and Holland ▷▷ *674*

[69] **300,000** Households with cable TV in UK

[70] **54** New roads started per year ▷▷ *578*

[71] **42** Percentage of households in Greater London with one car ▷▷ *1209*

[72] **64-68** Percentage of households in Greater London with one car officially forecast for 2001 ▷▷ *1293*

[73] **35,300** Average monthly registration of new cars in the year of Suez ▷▷ *1302*

[74] **184,200** Average monthly registration of new cars in 1988 ▷▷ *261*   ▷▷ *1303*

[75] **1,600,000** Annual car sales ▷▷ *1304*

[76] **£294,878,000** Car model advertising budgets in 1991 ▷▷ *306, 307*

[77] **£10,000,000** Value of GM Vauxhall's advertising campaign to launch its Astra model ◁◁ *10*   ▷▷ *88*

[78] **25** British children seriously injured by cars every day ▷▷ *90*

[79] **35,000** Tree-centuries of oxygen consumable by UK's 19m cars in a day ▷▷ *192*

[80] **40,000,000** Wattage of Toyota's Burnaston car plant ▷▷ *823*

[81] **2,000** Cars per week made at Nissan plant, Washington ▷▷ *824*

[82] **2,000** Miles driven by average Briton in 1970 ▷▷ *1209*

[83] **4,000** Miles driven by average Briton in 1989 ▷▷ *70* ▷▷ *427*   ▷▷ *1293*

[84] **60.4** Percentage of petrol price that is taxation in the UK ▷▷ *262*

[85] **24.2** Percentage of petrol price that is taxation in the USA ▷▷*795, 796*

[86] **30,000** Litres of water polluted to process components of one new car ▷▷*481*

[87] **310,000,000,000** Vehicle-kilometres travelled by UK cars in 1990 ▷▷*824*

[88] **540,000,000,000** Vehicle-kilometres forecast for UK cars in 2010

[89] **99,200** Ten- to 16-year-olds cautioned and found guilty of indictable offences each year ▷▷*718*

[90] **65** Child pedestrians injured each day in road accidents ▷▷*940*

[91] **1,914** Children aged five to nine killed or injured on the roads per year ▷▷*941*

[92] **1,000** Children deprived of their fathers each year by H M courts ▷▷*385*

[93] **7,038** Divorces in 1938 ▷▷*948*

[94] **164,105** Divorces in 1989 ▷▷*385*

[95] **£2,000,000,000** Backlog of repairs and maintenance on schools ▷▷*377*

[96] **102** Overall IQ of seven- to eight-year-olds in UK who were suckled in early life ◁◁*48*

[97] **92** Overall IQ of seven- to eight-year-olds in UK who were not suckled in early life ◁◁*47*

[98] **8.6** Percentage of Scottish children growing up in families dependent on DSS benefit in 1977 ▷▷*339*

[99] **20.4** Percentage of Scottish children growing up in families dependent on DSS benefit in 1990 ▷▷*479*

[100] **20** Percentage of women now aged 25 who will remain childless ▷▷*997*

[101] **96,400,000,000** Cigarettes smoked per year ▷▷*590, 591*

[102] **18,284** Miles British cigarettes produced on a typical working day would stretch laid butt-to-tip ▷▷*596, 597*

[103] **£30,000,000,000** Estimated value of clothing that sits unused in British wardrobes ▷▷*761*

[104] **2.9** Tonnes per person of greenhouse-effect carbon dioxide emitted annually in the UK ▷▷*212*

[105] **1.8** Tonnes per person of greenhouse-effect carbon dioxide emitted annually in Switzerland

[106] **872** Miles of nose-to-tail juggernaut loads of plastic computer casings used each year ▷▷*313*

[107] **68** Miles of nose-to-tail juggernaut loads of plastic containers made each year ▷▷*422, 423*   ▷▷*576*

[108] **1,000,000** Houses and businesses burgled per year ▷▷*718*

[109] **3,240** Incidence of the use of knives in assaults and robberies in the Metropolitan police district in 1980

[110] **7,500** Incidence of the use of knives in assaults and robberies in the Metropolitan police district in 1987 ▷▷*489, 490*

[111] **350 –700** Sentenced prisoners whose cases probation officers think should be reopened ▷▷*246, 247*

[112] **903** Knives seized at UK points of entry in 1990

[113] **2,082** Knives seized at UK points of entry in 1991 ▷▷*816*

[114] **952** Violent crimes in the London Borough of Newham in 1980

[115] **2,854** Violent crimes in the London Borough of Newham in 1991 ▷▷ *815, 816*

[116] **3,956,026** Convictions listed on the Police National Computer ▷▷ *322*

[117] **1:70** Proportion of prison population who were lifers in 1970

[118] **1:12.5** Proportion of prison population who were lifers in 1990 ▷▷ *489*

[119] **5,000** Composers who receive £250 to £5,000 a year from performance rights

[120] **9,960** Authors receiving £1 to £99 a year from public lending-library rights

[121] **1,561** Cinema screens in UK ▷▷ *122*

[122] **4,821** Cinema screens in France

[123] **1,900,000** Weekly UK cinema attendance

[124] **20,400,000** Weekly USA cinema attendance

[125] **2,421** Miles juggernauts would stretch loaded nose-to-tail with solid industrial waste authorised for dumping at sea by MAFF each year ▷▷ *243*

[126] **£24,000,000** Government propaganda budget 1979–80 ◁◁ *49*

[127] **£131,000,000** Government propaganda budget 1991–2 ▷▷ *426*

[128] **£62,000,000** Annual pay and expenses of UK military bands ▷▷ *129*

[129] **£32,000,000** Total annual taxpayer support for the national theatre companies

[130] **78** Percentage of professionals who take walks in the woods ▷▷*860*

[131] **32** Percentage of unskilled manual workers who take walks in the woods ▷▷*510*

[132] **£1,000,000,000** Annual budget of France's Ministry of Arts

[133] **£494,000,000** Annual budget of Britain's Ministry of Arts (Office of Arts and Libraries)

[134] **0** T-shirts allowed by treaty to be imported from Vietnam ▷▷*747*

[135] **5,539,000** T-shirts allowed by treaty to be imported from Thailand ▷▷*817*

[136] **0** Cycle lanes included in all tenderers' plans for second Severn Bridge ▷▷*1325*

[137] **£1,000** Estimated cost per mile of an urban cycle route ▷▷*1228*

[138] **£20,000,000** Average cost per mile of widening an urban road ◁◁*33*

[139] **10** Estimated miles of segregated highway cycle paths in Greater London ▷▷*1325*

[140] **118** Miles of London's M25 satellite motorway being widened ◁◁*73, 74*

[141] **£34,000,000** UK banks' private lending in 1966

[142] **£96,000,000,000** UK banks' private lending in 1991 ◁◁*43*

[143] **2** Number of times land occupied by the Ministry of Defence would accommodate the Yorkshire Dales National Park ▷▷ *702*

[144] **£60,600,000** Average annual aid to Bangladesh 1987–90

[145] **£71,100,000** Average annual spending on computers at the Ministry of Defence 1986–90 ▷▷ *889*

[146] **160** Staff employed by the Pesticide Safety Office ▷▷ *1079, 1080*

[147] **2,100** Staff employed by Directorate-General of Defence Accounts ▷▷ *248*

[148] **330** Spanish population per doctor ▷▷ *308, 309*

[149] **796** British population per doctor ▷▷ *285*

[150] **84** Percentage of annual drug convictions that are for personal possession of cannabis ▷▷ *179*

[151] **881** Olympic-sized swimming-pools of Scotch whisky produced on typical working day ◁◁ *58*   ▷▷ *559*

[152] **238,000,000** Litres of pure alcohol in the form of whisky exported per year ◁◁ *57*

[153] **400,000** Number of state-school teachers ▷▷ *374, 375*

[154] **400,000** Number of state-school administrators

[155] **24,372** Gigawatt hours of electricity generated in 1938 ◁◁ *73, 74*

[156] **286,275** Gigawatt hours of electricity generated in 1992 ◁◁ *80*

[157] **27** Percentage of households without central heating ▷▷ *1053*

[158] **1** Percentage of electricity produced by renewable means in the UK ▷▷*279, 280*

[159] **99** Percentage of electricity produced by renewable means in Norway ▷▷*274*

[160] **0.27** Energy consumption per Indian in average year (tonne/carbon equivalent) ▷▷*549*

[161] **5.36** Energy consumption per Briton in average year (tonne/carbon equivalent) ◁◁*82, 83*

[162] **£59,000,000** Budget of the Energy Efficiency Office ▷▷*844*

[163] **£40,000,000** Annual research-and-development budget of UK Nirex for nuclear waste disposal ▷▷*893*

[164] **289** UK industrial sites where an accident could cause a major public emergency ▷▷*499*

[165] **£27,900,000** Government expenditure on energy efficiency 1986–7 at 1989 prices

[166] **£15,000,000** Government expenditure on energy efficiency in 1989 ◁◁*162*

[167] **£24,500,000** Taxes spent on developing renewable forms of energy generation 1991–2 ▷▷*350*

[168] **1:113** Proportion of male Britons who are farmers ▷▷*1110*

[169] **£5,156** Minimum average per capita annual subsidy to Welsh full-time farmers ▷▷*526, 527*

[170] **£22,000,000** Grants and subsidies for hill livestock, sheep and suckler cows paid from Carlisle Ministry of Agriculture Office per year

[171] **£8,632** Agricultural worker's average annual income
▷▷*508*

[172] **196,400** Farmers, their partners and directors in 1979

[173] **179,500** Farmers, their partners and directors in 1991
▷▷*180*

[174] **61** Average acreage of UK farms ▷▷*1038*

[175] **2.9** Average acreage of Japanese farms ▷▷*259, 260*

[176] **12** Percentage of women who are obese
▷▷*597*

[177] **1,136** Average tonnes of annual decline in UK scampi
catch since 1988 ◁◁*125*

[178] **24** Miles of nose-to-tail juggernaut loads of parsnips
produced each year by UK farmers

[179] **£13,000,000,000** Spending on alcoholic drinks per year
▷▷*233*

[180] **201,923** Football fields of farmland to be set aside
unfarmed in a country (UK) which imports 46.6 per cent of
its food and feedstuffs ▷▷*1098*

[181] **10,000** Free-range eggs consumed in the House of
Commons each week ◁◁*19*

[182] **87** Average lbs of beef, lamb and pork consumed
annually per Briton ▷▷*1072, 1073*   ▷▷*1116, 1117*

[183] **23,049** Cases of 'mad cow disease' ▷▷*571, 572*

[184] **5,600,000** Estimated number of vegetarians and limited
meat-eaters ▷▷*571*

[185] **£30,000,000** Sales of organic fruit and vegetables in
1989 ▷▷*284*

[186] **£82,000,000** Sales of organic fruit and vegetables
    predicted for 1993

[187] **18** Lbs of plastic food and drink packaging used per
    Briton per year ▷▷*318*

[188] **186** Miles juggernauts would stretch nose-to-tail loaded
    with a year's plastic packaging for British food and drink
    ◁◁*107*

[189] **107** Kilos of potatoes per Briton produced by UK farmers
    each year ◁◁*176*

[190] **500** Tonnes of Third World tea upon which boiling British
    water is poured each day ▷▷*889*

[191] **46.6** Percentage of UK's food and feedstuffs that is
    imported ◁◁*180*   ▷▷*310*

[192] **121** UK's rank among 140 countries for percentage of
    land under forests ◁◁*46*   ▷▷*291*

[193] **7** Percentage of the UK covered by forest

[194] **72** Percentage of Colombia, South America, covered by
    forest ▷▷*890*

[195] **27,000** Acres of woodland in Oxfordshire

[196] **111** Acres of woodland in Oxfordshire with public access
    ◁◁*130, 131*

[197] **293,846** Football fields of public forest sold off in the
    Thatcher years ◁◁*59*

[198] **143** Kilometres of nose-to-tail juggernauts of freight
    hauled per average Briton in 1978 ▷▷*261*

[199] **177** Kilometres of nose-to-tail juggernauts of freight
    hauled per average Briton in 1988 ▷▷*364, 365*

[200] **4,500,000,000** Kilometres of nose-to-tail juggernauts of freight in 1978 ▷▷*261*

[201] **5,740,000,000** Kilometres of nose-to-tail juggernauts of freight in 1991 ▷▷*402*

[202] **46** Percentage increase in tonnage moved by juggernaut lorries since 1980 ▷▷*401*   ▷▷*436*   ▷▷*441, 442*

[203] **36** Percentage of road-freight deliveries made out of normal working hours ▷▷*436*

[204] **340** Kilowatts per hour used by UK refrigerators

[205] **60** Kilowatt consumption if up-to-date types of refrigerator were used ▷▷*769, 770*

[206] **17** Number of pesticide residues found in officially tested strawberries ▷▷*1048, 1049*

[207] **£20,444** The Department of Energy's 1989/90 gas bill in constant sterling

[208] **£49,763** The Department of Energy's 1990/91 gas bill in constant sterling ◁◁*162, 163*

[209] **5.6** Tonnes of glass recycled annually per 1,000 people in Britain

[210] **13** Tonnes of glass recycled annually per 1,000 people in France ▷▷*293, 294*

[211] **19,865** Miles juggernauts would stretch nose-to-tail loaded with glass fibre consumed each year in the UK ▷▷*312*

[212] **586,666** Road tankers of carbon dioxide that could be removed annually from the atmosphere by construction of a Severn barrage for power generation ◁◁*162, 163*

[213] **34** Officially identified tidal barrage sites for power generation ▷▷*279, 280*

[214] **257,222** Tonnes of agricultural methane gas emitted each year ▷▷ *1017*

[215] **42,000** Tonnes of major climate-changing pollutants emitted on average day in the UK ▷▷ *916, 917*

[216] **90,980** Canned drinks sold per year at the House of Commons ▷▷ *355*

[217] **0** Can recycling units at House of Commons ◁◁ *125*

[218] **£73,000** Cost of launch party for the Prime Minister's Citizen's Charter

[219] **171,309** Number of individual government forms for business that were reviewed for effectiveness 1982–90 ▷▷ *1447*

[220] **31** Publications per average working day of Her Majesty's Stationery Office ▷▷ *879*

[221] **59,800** Staff of the Inland Revenue ▷▷ *856*

[222] **£5.50** Cost of administering each weekly £66.95 married-couple unemployment-benefit payment ◁◁ *39*

[223] **£68,000,000** Department of Education office costs 1988–9 ▷▷ *153, 154*

[224] **£98,000,000** Department of Education office costs 1991–2 ▷▷ *153, 154*

[225] **£105,000** Annual security-company contracts of the Welsh Office

[226] **£3,284,659** Annual security-company contracts of the Northern Ireland Office ◁◁ *15*

[227] **500** Average number of ships negotiating the Straits of Dover at any given time ▷▷ *1287*

[228] **75** Percentage of people who put environmental protection ahead of economic growth ▷▷*592, 593*

[229] **14** UK nuclear-bomb tests since 1980 ▷▷*911*

[230] **6,000,000** People treated for clinical mental illness per year ▷▷*233*

[231] **£35** Cost of drugs per person, including children, budgeted annually for NHS family doctors ◁◁*179* ▷▷*308*

[232] **54** Percentage of adults not taking any form of exercise ◁◁*176*

[233] **88,461** Prescriptions of benzodiazepine tranquilliser drugs in UK per weekday ▷▷*560*   ▷▷*1097*

[234] **4,000** Estimated miles of hedgerows destroyed per year ◁◁*8*   ▷▷*1098*

[235] **2,005,000** Number of dwellings in a 'poor' environment ▷▷*828*   ▷▷*909*

[236] **39,000** Tonnes of expanded polystyrene housing and packaging materials made per year ▷▷*315*   ▷▷*709*

[237] **20,000** Hostel beds in London ▷▷*828*

[238] **6** Unoccupied royal palaces in London ▷▷*813*

[239] **£29,000,000** Housing benefit paid in Tower Hamlets, Greater London in 1985–6

[240] **£57,400,000** Housing benefit paid in Tower Hamlets, Greater London in 1990–91 ◁◁*55*   ◁◁*56*

[241] **£21,941,375** Treasury support of immigrant services of Inner London Education Authority in 1990 ◁◁*59*

[242] **90,000** Residents of Macao potentially eligible to immigrate to UK in 1993

[243] **25,000** Number of times articulated road tankers loaded nose-to-tail with one year's UK liquid industrial effluent would circle the globe ▷▷ *1428*

[244] **1** Number of British Airways flights taking off or landing per minute, 24 hours a day, 365 days a year ▷▷ *892*

[245] **11** Convictions for insider trading during the 1980s ◁◁ *59*

[246] **19,225** Prison staff in England and Wales in 1974 ▷▷ *266, 267*

[247] **31,863** Prison staff in England and Wales in 1989 ◁◁ *117, 118*

[248] **208,320** Football fields of farmland run by the Ministry of Defence ◁◁ *174*

[249] **84** Hyde Parks of vacant land in the metropolitan counties ▷▷ *1037*

[250] **293** Hyde Parks of land left derelict by industry ▷▷ *1036*

[251] **£2,000,000** Cost per square metre of attempting to reconstruct peat bog ▷▷ *1041, 1042*

[252] **241** Hyde Parks of underused or unused public land on the Land Register ▷▷ *1037*

[253] **4,000** UK houses owned by people with estates worth over £2,000,000 ▷▷ *722*

[254] **11,324** Football fields of land left derelict by excavations and pits ▷▷ *1036*

[255] **5,000** Number of individuals owning three-quarters of Britain's land in the 1890s ▷▷ *722*

[256] **6,000,000** Households numbering one person ◁◁ *93, 94*   ▷▷ *338*

[257] **30.4** Percentage of Scottish households consisting of one adult ▷▷*545*

[258] **56** Mental handicap and illness hospitals to be closed by 1994 ◁◁*230*

[259] **255,128** Mopeds in Britain ▷▷*1377, 1378*

[260] **13,903,572** Mopeds in Japan ▷▷*1407*

[261] **39** Percentage of England's motorway system being widened ▷▷*1284*

[262] **2,480** Extra miles of major roads and motorways built in last 10 years ▷▷*877*

[263] **6,900** Vehicles per kilometre of UK motorway ▷▷*869* ▷▷*1162*

[264] **£39,960** Staff allowances for MPs

[265] **£250,000** Staff allowances for US federal legislators ▷▷*856*

[266] **299** Men in prison for killing their spouse or lover ▷▷*385*

[267] **22** Women in prison for killing their spouse or lover ▷▷*718*

[268] **3,116,300** Admissions to the Science Museum in London in 1987

[269] **1,121,100** Admissions to the Science Museum in London in 1989, after entry charges were introduced

[270] **12,000** High estimate of users injecting drugs in Glasgow area ▷▷*827*

[271] **£9,080,000** Subsidy for treating English road-accident victims in hospital each year ◁◁*262*

[272] **143,476** Football fields of Welsh sheep farms still under post-Chernobyl irradiation restrictions ▷▷ *350*

[273] **10** Rough percentage of private electricity bills donated to nuclear industry ◁◁ *158*

[274] **13** French nuclear-power reactors within 85 miles of British coast ▷▷ *1395*

[275] **69** Olympic-sized swimming-pools of 'hot' nuclear waste left from all US nuclear-weapon production ▷▷ *1297*

[276] **30** Olympic-sized swimming-pools of nuclear waste from foreign spent fuel reprocessed at Sellafield and Dounreay ▷▷ *279*   ▷▷ *794*

[277] **181** Tonnes of spent uranium shipped into the UK since 1965 ▷▷ *893*

[278] **1,269** Cubic metres of 'intermediate waste' generated at Sellafield reprocessing plant in a year ◁◁ *26*

[279] **£18,000,000** Annual taxes spent on researching renewable forms of energy

[280] **£137,000,000** Annual taxes spent on researching nuclear-fission energy

[281] **8,000** Annual flights over the UK carrying radioactive materials ▷▷ *892*

[282] **27,000** Oil tankers docking in UK ports annually ◁◁ *227*

[283] **44,000** NHS operations carried out per week

[284] **75** Percentage of organic fruit and vegetables that is imported ◁◁ *206*

[285] **36,058,803** Outpatients treated by the NHS per year

[286] **0** Department of Health officials working full-time on the human health effect of ozone-layer depletion ▷▷*892*

[287] **68** Percentage increase in registered Scottish cases of malignant skin cancer annually 1980–89 ▷▷*892*

[288] **£4,700,000,000** Turnover of food packager Dalgety plc in 1989 ▷▷*853*

[289] **$211,500,000** UK sales of analgesic pain-killers per year ▷▷*559*   ▷▷*662*

[290] **$68,000,000** France's sales of analgesic pain-killers per year

[291] **159** Tonnes of House of Commons printed paper used in a Parliamentary session ▷▷*1450*

[292] **627** Miles of nose-to-tail juggernaut loads of newsprint imported per year ▷▷*504, 505*   ▷▷*1487*

[293] **671** Tonnes of paper recycled annually per 1,000 population in Belgium

[294] **52** Tonnes of paper recycled annually per 1,000 population in UK ▷▷*879*

[295] **40** Juggernaut loads of toilet paper flushed away each day in Britain ▷▷*479*

[296] **19,710/19,932** UK's patent applications in 1980 and 1989

[297] **165,730/317,353** Japan's patent applications in 1980 and 1989 ▷▷*750*

[298] **5,000** People in England and Wales suffering acute pesticide poisoning annually ▷▷*883*

[299] **211** Agricultural premises covered by each government Health and Safety Inspector

[300] **1,800** Juggernaut loads of neat chemicals spread on British farms each year ▷▷*818*   ▷▷*1165*

[301] **700,000** Dead animals disposed of each year by knackers and hunt kennels ◁◁*26*

[302] **£20,800,000** Petrol and oil advertising budgets in 1988 ▷▷*1284*

[303] **£26,900,000** Petrol and oil advertising budgets in 1989 ▷▷*374*   ▷▷*870*

[304] **50** Kilograms of petroleum used annually by average Pakistani

[305] **1,724** Kilograms of petroleum used annually by average Briton ▷▷*1025*

[306] **39** British petroleum consumption in the year of the Suez crisis (statistical units)

[307] **116** British petroleum consumption in 1988 (statistical units) ▷▷*543*

[308] **1,414** Adverse drug reactions reported in NHS in 1964

[309] **19,246** Adverse drug reactions reported in NHS in 1989 ▷▷*560*

[310] **1,038** Miles of nose-to-tail juggernaut loads of plastics materials imported per year ▷▷*315*   ▷▷*321*

[311] **1,397** Juggernaut loads of plasticised PVC film and sheet, including cling film, produced each year ▷▷*320* ▷▷*1450*

[312] **3,965** Plastics processing plants in the UK ▷▷*1428* ▷▷*1451*

[313] **174** Miles juggernauts would stretch nose-to-tail loaded with a year's production of polyethylene film and sheeting for products such as plastic bags ▷▷*1430*

[314] **5,031** Juggernaut loads of PVC doors and windows made per year ▷▷ *1422, 1423*

[315] **20,000,000** Tonnes of hardwood required annually for charcoal to smelt Amazon pig iron used in UK and EC car manufacture ◁◁ *140*   ▷▷ *1414*

[316] **34,000** Plastic bottles required to make one tonne of plastic scrap ▷▷ *517*   ▷▷ *1460*

[317] **1–2** Percentage of all used plastic consumer packaging that is recycled ◁◁ *312*   ▷▷ *1459*

[318] **559** Miles of nose-to-tail juggernaut loads of plastic packaging produced each year ▷▷ *355*

[319] **1,200,000** Used plastic office machine toner cartridges dumped in UK landfill sites each year ▷▷ *1447*

[320] **600** Tonnes of plastic waste saved a year by Sainsbury supermarkets reducing the size of their tear-off fruit and vegetable bags

[321] **208** Tonnes of Britain's 455,000 annual tonnage of household plastic packaging that is recycled ◁◁ *63*

[322] **5,399,382** Criminal names on the Police National Computer ▷▷ *744, 745*

[323] **2,900** Road-tanker loads of domestic bleach flushed away each year ▷▷ *1425*

[324] **4** Percentage of people unconcerned about pollution ▷▷ *1483*

[325] **40** Percentage of colds and sore throats occurring in summer months ▷▷ *560*

[326] **164** Tonnes of sulphur dioxide emitted by UK road vehicles every day ▷▷ *667, 668*

[327] **2,087** Tonnes of volatile organic compounds emitted by UK traffic every day ◁◁*87*

[328] **35** Grams of carbon monoxide emitted per juggernaut-kilometre of freight ◁◁*198, 199* ▷▷*329*

[329] **1.50** Grams of carbon monoxide emitted per juggernaut-kilometre of freight carried by rail ▷▷*342, 343*

[330] **15,756** Tonnes of carbon monoxide emitted by UK road vehicles every day ◁◁*82, 83* ▷▷*435*

[331] **4** Percentage reduction in annual carbon-dioxide emissions expected from new MOT exhaust checks ▷▷*443*

[332] **£122,000** Works budget on House of Commons and House of Lords each working day

[333] **£35,000** Research and monitoring budget of H M Inspectorate of Pollution each working day in 1993/4 ▷▷*437*

[334] **12** British government traffic air-pollution monitoring units ◁◁*892*

[335] **200** German government traffic air-pollution monitoring units

[336] **12.5** Percentage of Welsh residents among British mainland population in 1891

[337] **2.5** Percentage of Welsh residents among British mainland population in 1991

[338] **£35,000,000,000** Government's annual income-support budget for the elderly

[339] **£616,000,000,000** Government's annual dole budget ▷▷*804*

[340] **280,000** Families on family credit payments in 1988–9

[341] **430,000** Families expected to be on £48 per week family credit payments in 1993–4 ◁◁*54*

[342] **5,230** Road transport fatalities per year ◁◁*91*

[343] **31** Rail passenger fatalities per year

[344] **6,501** Passengers killed or injured on the railways per year

[345] **9,292** Passengers killed or injured on buses and coaches per year ▷▷*689*

[346] **26** Average age of British Rail's non-Intercity locomotives

[347] **12,200,000** Reduction in annual Scottish rail passengers 1985–90 ◁◁*75*

[348] **17** Average age of British Rail's non-Intercity passenger coaches ◁◁*76*

[349] **2,000,000** Hardwood doors imported from tropical countries per year ▷▷*1175, 1176*

[350] **20** Years UK Magnox nuclear reactors, first installed in 1965, were designed to last ▷▷*544*

[351] **8.7** Tonnes of aluminium recycled annually per 1,000 population in Holland

[352] **4.0** Tonnes of aluminium recycled annually per 1,000 population in the UK ▷▷*533*   ▷▷*535*

[353] **13,163** UK citizens per available bottle bank ▷▷*587, 588*   ▷▷*658*

[354] **267,000** Population per recycling or waste-reclaiming business in Greater London ▷▷*476, 477*   ▷▷*1472*

[355] **8,280,000,000** British steel cans dumped, littered or burnt per year ▷▷ *1216*

[356] **6** Percentage of Americans who say they have no religion

[357] **34** Percentage of Britons who say they have no religion ◁◁*93, 94*

[358] **ECU201** Per capita research-and-development funds in France

[359] **ECU128** Per capita research-and-development funds in the UK ◁◁*279, 280*

[360] **9,002** Miles of freshwater rivers and canals with fair to bad water quality ▷▷ *1105* ▷▷ *1483*

[361] **£1,000,000,000** The taxpayer's motorway and trunk-road building budget 1988/9 ◁◁*306, 307* ▷▷ *1284*

[362] **£2,117,000,000** The taxpayer's motorway and trunk-road building budget in 1993/4 ◁◁*304, 305*

[363] **£5,100,000** Public expenditure on new road construction every working day ▷▷*687* ▷▷*877*

[364] **65,000** Secret companies registered in the British Virgin Islands in 1992 ▷▷ *722*

[365] **£4** Ford Motor Company's reported 1989 charitable giving per employee ▷▷ *1413, 1414*

[366] **£27,423** Taxpayers' weekly expenditure on the royal train ▷▷ *720*

[367] **£23,250** Average annual household income where both partners work ▷▷ *782*

[368] **£843** Cost of the royal flowers per week ▷▷*510* ▷▷ *782*

[369] **£493,269** Average tax expenditure on royal-family housing per week ◁◁*13*

[370] **£224** Average household expenditure per week

[371] **740** Annual kilos of municipal waste per American

[372] **360** Annual kilos of municipal waste per Briton ▷▷*1472*

[373] **35** Percentage of 16-year-olds attending school ◁◁*89*

[374] **£12,597,120** Annual government grant for state-school textbooks in 1988–9 in constant sterling

[375] **£10,800,000** Annual government grant for state-school textbooks in 1989–90 in constant sterling ◁◁*777, 778*

[376] **21.7** Percentage of school-leavers with no graded result in the London Borough of Newham 1990 ◁◁*114,115*

[377] **39** Percentage of Manchester school-leavers with no English CSE 1987–8 ◁◁*92* ▷▷*1014*

[378] **1,780,000** Surplus places in English schools ▷▷*1015*

[379] **£15,000,000** Annual government grant for state-school textbooks in 1990–91 in constant sterling

[380] **£19,182,894** Annual government grant for state-school textbooks in 1987–8 in constant sterling

[381] **−3** Percentage change in book sales to schools since 1985 at real prices ◁◁*30*

[382] **13** Security-firm officers employed by the Department of Energy in 1985 ◁◁*225, 226*

[383] **74** Security-firm officers employed by the Department of Energy in 1991 ◁◁*15*

[384] **1,090,910** Juggernaut loads of sewage sludge dumped
at sea or spread on agricultural land each year ◁◁*323*
▷▷*1485*   ▷▷*1488*

[385] **78,468** Couples with children who divorce per year
▷▷*718*

[386] **2,461** Abortions per working day ▷▷*966*

[387] **28** Percentage of women who say they had their best
kiss over 10 years ago

[388] **186,000** Babies born to unmarried mothers per year
◁◁*94*   ▷▷*888*

[389] **2,000,000** Pornographic magazines sold each month
▷▷*489, 490*   ▷▷*669*

[390] **750,000,000** Sanitary pads disposed of each year
◁◁*46*   ▷▷*488*   ▷▷*1190*

[391] **33,000** Non-specific genital infections in women in 1981
▷▷*395*   ▷▷*719*

[392] **48,000** Non-specific genital infections in women in 1988
▷▷*396, 397*

[393] **43,000** Male cases of gonorrhoea in 1971

[394] **12,000** Male cases of gonorrhoea in 1988 ◁◁*285*

[395] **95** Percentage of the sexually active who find intercourse
very or fairly satisfying

[396] **58** Percentage of people in the Midlands who find sex
very satisfying

[397] **47** Percentage of people in the South who find sex very
satisfying

[398] **£2,000,000** Taxes allocated to solar-power research
1991–2 ◁◁*279*   ▷▷*399*   ▷▷*829*

[399] **£94,100,000** Taxes allocated to nuclear power research 1991–2 ▷▷ *544*

[400] **400** Microspecies of wild blackberry growing in British fields ◁◁*6*

[401] **41,477** Miles juggernauts would stretch loaded nose-to-tail with stone quarried for motorways, trunk and local roads each year ▷▷ *1036*

[402] **217,000** Miles of nose-to-tail juggernauts of stone aggregate required for the government's road-building plans ▷▷ *1036*

[403] **1,162** Miles nose-to-tail juggernaut loads of aggregate mined, processed and trucked for rail lines each year would stretch ◁◁*347*

[404] **£986,000,000** EC subsidies to sugar farming in 1990 ▷▷ *526*

[405] **16.5** Percentage profit margin of British Sugar 1990–1

[406] **1,500** Reported male suicides per year

[407] **328** Reported female suicides per year

[408] **24** Average weekly hours of TV viewing per person ◁◁*379* ◁◁*380, 381*

[409] **9.2** Years spent watching TV in child's 65-year remaining life ▷▷ *412* ▷▷ *864, 865*

[410] **340** Typical colour TV's electricity consumption in kilowatt-hours per year ◁◁*901* ▷▷ *1233*

[411] **70** Best available colour TV's electricity consumption in kilowatt-hours per year ▷▷ *444, 445*

[412] **97** Percentage of UK homes equipped with television ▷▷ *627* ▷▷ *669*

[413] **35** Percentage of state schoolboys attaining A–C grade (G)CSE in English

[414] **£2,400,000** Taxpayer funding for proof-of-concept of HOTOL aeroplane

[415] **£205,000** Taxpayer funding for UK's first shoreline wave-energy system ▷▷ *1395*

[416] **5** Applications to export manufactured leg-irons (oversized cuffs) per year ▷▷ *889*

[417] **3,000** Pesticide products available ◁◁ *64*   ▷▷ *642*

[418] **1,672** Juggernaut loads of hazardous wastes imported by transfrontier shipment each year ▷▷ *681*

[419] **451,600** Cleveland's 1989 tonnage of toxic or hazardous waste production ▷▷ *716*

[420] **119,178** Cleveland's 1985 tonnage of toxic or hazardous waste production ▷▷ *716*

[421] **919** Miles of nose-to-tail juggernaut loads of hazardous waste disposed of by local authorities each year ◁◁ *125*

[422] **199,486** Tonnes of pure carcinogenic benzene exported per year ▷▷ *1462*

[423] **90,200** Tonnes of pure carcinogenic benzene imported per year ▷▷ *1466*

[424] **702** Miles of nose-to-tail juggernaut loads of toxic waste produced by UK industry in 1986–7

[425] **860** Miles of nose-to-tail juggernaut loads of toxic waste produced by UK industry in 1990–91

[426] **£99,000,000** Government's total advertising spend per year

[427] **5,000** Tonnes of litter collected per year by seaside village resort Torbay's district council ▷▷ *543*

[428] **39,567,000** Registered vehicle keepers on the Police National Computer ▷▷ *1284*   ▷▷ *1288*

[429] **18,600,000** Number of vehicles on UK roads in 1980

[430] **24,510,607** Latest number of vehicles on UK roads ▷▷ *728*

[431] **£1,000,000** Estimated increase in the Isle of Wight's annual revenues if it imposed a universal 40-mph speed limit ◁◁ *271*   ▷▷ *916, 917*

[432] **43** Percentage increase in heavy-lorry use of minor roads since 1973 ◁◁ *202, 203*

[433] **10.2** Average morning peak traffic speed in mph in Greater London ▷▷ *689*

[434] **1,000,000** People estimated to be regularly cycling to work ◁◁ *137, 138*

[435] **14,500,000,000** Average annual increase in passenger kilometres travelled by car, taxi and motorcycle between 1978 and 1988 ▷▷ *1284*   ▷▷ *1350*

[436] **34** Percentage increase in UK juggernaut-lorry traffic since 1980 ▷▷ *655, 656*

[437] **606,000** Air hours flown by commercial aircraft over British air space in 1987 ▷▷ *892*

[438] **706,000** Air hours flown by commercial aircraft over British air space in 1989 ◁◁ *244*   ▷▷ *549*

[439] **£391,000,000** Taxpayer grant to London Regional Transport in 1986

[440] **£287,000,000** Taxpayer grant to London Regional Transport in 1990 ◁◁ *71*

[441] **19,071** 38-tonne juggernauts licensed in 1984

[442] **50,453** 38-tonne juggernauts licensed in 1988
▷▷*696, 697*

[443] **2,000,000,000** Extra trees needed to absorb most of
Britain's carbon dioxide emissions ▷▷*1413, 1414*

[444] **£3,450,000** TV advertising expenditure per day in France

[445] **£6,000,000** TV advertising expenditure per day in UK
▷▷*1496*

[446] **1,000,000** Reduction in number of people aged 16 –19
years between 1984 and 1994 ▷▷*987*

[447] **978,000** Estimated increase in UK population since 1981
▷▷*997*   ▷▷*1000*

[448] **10,400,000** Population of UK at its foundation in 1801
▷▷*950*

[449] **4,000,000** UK population increase since 1961 ▷▷*1005*

[450] **465** Daily increase in the mainland British population
since 1891 ▷▷*946*

[451] **£11,700,000,000** Cost to taxpayer of developing UK
sections of Tornado fighter (not including radar) ▷▷*565*
▷▷*1264*

[452] **£6,507,000** Cost of operating British Army of the Rhine
each working day ◁◁*145*

[453] **20** Percentage of taxation going to the Ministry of
Defence ▷▷*557*

[454] **£667,000,000** Budget of 'other MOD TLBs' (secret
defence agencies) annually ▷▷*566*

[455] **95** States to which the Ministry of Defence provides
military training ▷▷*791*

[456] **11,734** Ministry of Defence staff dedicated to weapons research ◁◁*165* ▷▷*565*

[457] **10,111** Military married quarters vacant ◁◁*258*

[458] **7,192** Written enquiries or complaints to Whitehall about low-flying military aircraft per year ◁◁*451* ▷▷*892*

[459] **175,000** Average-priced houses that could be built by abolishing Trident submarine nuclear-war system ◁◁*239, 240*

[460] **£230,000,000,000** Estimated cost of UK's Trident nuclear-war system over 20 years

[461] **20,000** Hiroshimas the UK's planned four Trident submarines could destroy ◁◁*128* ▷▷*466, 467*

[462] **£264** Depreciation cost of driving a Challenger tank one mile ◁◁*455*

[463] **67** Number of US military bases in the UK ◁◁*457* ▷▷*565*

[464] **$299,355,000,000** The USA's defence budget ▷▷*566*

[465] **$345,000,000,000** Entire UK government annual budget

[466] **447** Vessels in Royal Navy in 1960

[467] **173** Vessels in Royal Navy in 1990

[468] **25,000** Supertankers of waste produced a year in UK ◁◁*419* ▷▷*476, 477*

[469] **3** Number of times clinical waste produced annually in Greater London would fill Trafalgar Square to the height of Nelson's Column ▷▷*486*

[470] **170,000** Tonnes of clinical waste burned annually in 600 hospital incinerators ▷▷ *709*

[471] **130** Estimated grams of dioxins emitted by hospital incinerators each year ◁◁ *48*

[472] **1,092** Juggernaut loads of waste produced from UK industrial processes each working hour ▷▷ *1351*

[473] **40,000** Items of space-junk in orbit ▷▷ *899*

[474] **4,504** Juggernaut loads of polystyrene packaging produced each year ▷▷ *1451*

[475] **3,818** Juggernaut loads of PET/PBT plastic consumed each year making such products as recyclable plastic bottles ▷▷ *1460*

[476] **£83,000,000** Current budget for national waste and recycling initiatives ◁◁ *371, 372*

[477] **£57,000,000** Budget for national waste and recycling initiatives in 1993/4 ◁◁ *418*

[478] **£74,200,000** Annual sales of household bin liners ▷▷ *1430*

[479] **53** Percentage of Scotland's sewage discharged with no treatment at all ▷▷ *870*   ▷▷ *1474*

[480] **383** Tonnes of washing-up liquid produced each UK working day ▷▷ *1425*

[481] **£127,900,000** City firms' fees paid by taxpayer for water privatisation ▷▷ *1428*

[482] **9,200,000** Champagne imports by bottle in 1979

[483] **22,700,000** Champagne imports by bottle in 1989 ▷▷ *508*

[484] **0** Women who have served on the government's Advisory Commission on Advertising since 1980 ▷▷*486*

[485] **35** Average number of beatings a battered wife sustains before seeking help ▷▷*489*

[486] **6** Women chairpersons of any of the 40 committees under the Department of Health during the premiership of Mrs Thatcher ▷▷*719*

[487] **0** Women chairing any of the 43 public bodies under the Department of the Environment after a decade of Mrs Thatcher's premiership ◁◁*228*

[488] **14,000,000** Menstruating women in the UK ◁◁*390* ▷▷*662*

[489] **507** English and Welsh Crown Court sentences for indecent assault on a female in 1980

[490] **1,431** English and Welsh Crown Court sentences for indecent assault on a female in 1990 ◁◁*389*

[491] **590,000** One-parent benefit recipients in 1985–6

[492] **825,000** Recipients of £5.60 one-parent benefit expected in 1993–4 ▷▷*961*

[493] **443,000** Number of females with a degree in 1979 ◁◁*487*

[494] **931,000** Number of females with a degree in 1989 ◁◁*486*

[495] **2.3** Percentage of graded diplomatic staff in the Foreign Office who are women ◁◁*486*

[496] **46.8** Percentage of all diplomatic staff in the Foreign Office who are women

[497] **357,000** Women self-employed in 1979 ▷▷*498*

[498] **782,000** Women self-employed in 1989 ◁◁*221*

[499] **262** Typical annual total of fatal workplace accidents on Wednesdays ▷▷*1089*

[500] **99** Typical annual total of fatal workplace accidents on Fridays ▷▷*686*

[501] **£6,526** Pay of average US corporate boss per working day ◁◁*171*

[502] **£122.50** Revised top daily-pay rate of hospital trainee doctor ▷▷*508*   ▷▷*1218*

[503] **1,000,000** Number of people usually off work each day ◁◁*499*

[504] **£7,923** Reported income of *Sunday Sport*'s publisher per working day ◁◁*389*   ◁◁*489, 490*

[505] **£25** Basic income of a British Army private soldier per day ▷▷*1450*

[506] **£10** Daily-pay rate of a 16-year-old casual farm worker ▷▷*1141*

[507] **1,000,000** Taxpayers with incomes from £30,000 to £40,000 ▷▷*889*

[508] **£3,068** Typical daily-pay rate of a chairman of a merchant bank ▷▷*782*

[509] **£21,865** Weekly-pay increase of head of Tesco supermarkets in 1991 ▷▷*703*

[510] **£4** Real-terms increase of lowest-paid tenth of male manual workers during decade 1982–92 ◁◁*506*

[511] **£305,000,000** Taxpayers' annual bill per 100,000 unemployed ▷▷*512*

[512] **£315,256,000** Taxes raised from all pools betting per year ◁◁*511*

[513] **44** Percentage of remand inmates surveyed who said they were unemployed prior to imprisonment

[514] **500,000** UK jobs dependent on war industries ◁◁*451*

[515] **11** Hectares per worker on 420-hectare farm in 1885

[516] **37** Hectares per worker on 420-hectare farm in 1970 ▷▷*1165*

[517] **0.1** Percentage of plastic bottles which are recycled ◁◁*475* ▷▷*1466*

▶ ▶FIRST CLASS ZONE

[518] **82** Percentage of Poland's forests showing signs of pollution damage ▷▷ *1292*   ▷▷ *1397*

[519] **9,000** Dead lakes in former East Germany ▷▷ *648* ▷▷ *1315*

[520] **70.4** Life expectancy of a Russian in 1963−4 ▷▷ *975, 976, 978*

[521] **69.3** Life expectancy of a Russian in 1990

[522] **$990,000,000** US sales of disposable incontinency pads in 1990

[523] **$2,230,000,000** US sales of disposable incontinency pads expected in 1995 ◁◁ *3*   ▷▷ *978*

[524] **36** Percentage loss of agricultural production predicted for Greece by one degree centigrade of global warming ▷▷ *1302*

[525] **£120** Per acre grant to Danish farmers to go organic ▷▷ *1079*

[526] **£1,153,846** EC weekly subsidies to rice growers ◁◁ *170*   ▷▷ *657*

[527] **35,211** Tonnes of rice produced in the EC per week

[528] **27** Miles juggernauts would stretch nose-to-tail loaded with cereal food aid granted to Ethiopia in 1991

[529] **8,608** Miles juggernauts would stretch nose-to-tail loaded with cereal in the Euro-cereal mountain ◁◁ *234*   ▷▷ *706*

[530] **11** Percentage of chemical fertiliser production that is lost on the way to fields of former Soviet Union ▷▷ *1041, 1042*

[531] **38** Percentage increase in US internal air cargo 1984–9 ▷▷ *1162*

[532] **89** Percentage increase in US international air cargo 1984–9 ◁◁*244*

[533] **19** Kilograms of aluminium waste annually per West European

[534] **4** Kilograms of aluminium waste recycled per Briton ◁◁*351, 352*

[535] **8.6** Kilograms of aluminium waste recycled per West German

[536] **53** Animal species made extinct over the last 100 years in Hungary ▷▷*1186*

[537] **7** Olympic-sized swimming-pools of gas that represents each American's energy use per year ◁◁*207, 208*

[538] **11.8** Euro-states' birthrate per 1,000 population ▷▷*539*   ▷▷*996*

[539] **15.9** USA's birthrate per 1,000 population

[540] **600** Tonnes of lead wastes poured into the Black Sea per year ▷▷*904*

[541] **1,300** Cars per 1,000 households in Italy ▷▷*746*   ▷▷*1252*

[542] **200,000** Parking spaces destined for removal in Paris ▷▷*1400*   ▷▷*1413, 1414*

[543] **4,050** Supertankers of water polluted during the manufacture of the 13,500,000 new cars sold each year in Western Europe ▷▷*1489*

[544] **20** Percentage of Byelorussian farmland rendered unusable by radiation from the Chernobyl disaster ◁◁*274*   ▷▷*1268*

[545] **62** Percentage of EC households not containing anyone aged under 15 ▷▷*731*   ▷▷*945*

[546] **265,696** Youths drafted for military service in France each year

[547] **69,000** Estimated tonnes of major climate-changing pollutants emitted on an average day in Germany ▷▷ *700*

[548] **436** Football fields of microcomputer screens in US homes ▷▷ *1243*

[549] **3** Road tankers of jet fuel burned by a 17-year-old Concorde supersonic airliner on a London–New York flight ◁◁ *244*   ▷▷ *892*

[550] **0.5** Estimated grams of carcinogenic petrochemicals ingested each day by a typical Briton ▷▷ *1413, 1414*

[551] **1,108,100** Tonnes of ozone-layer-destroying nitrogen oxides emitted each year by UK road transport ▷▷ *1409, 1410*

[552] **£3,400,000,000** Architectural budget of large public cultural buildings in Paris over the last decade

[553] **54** Nationalities at a high school in Seine-St-Denis, France ▷▷ *889*

[554] **145** Radio stations in the UK

[555] **2,500** Radio stations in Italy

[556] **62.6** US Pentagon research-and-development budget as a percentage of government appropriations ▷▷ *565*

[557] **5.5** Percentage of US gross national product spent on defence ▷▷ *791*   ▷▷ *912*

[558] **228,235** Guided missiles procured by the US Pentagon 1989–91 ▷▷ *763*

[559] **$10.14** Spending on pain-killers per American each year ◁◁ *289, 290*   ▷▷ *1094*

[560] **$4,000,000** Spent each day by Europeans on over-the-counter pain-killers ◁◁*308*

[561] **30,346** Miles juggernauts loaded with one year's Canadian coal output would stretch nose-to-tail ▷▷*915* ▷▷*1342* ▷▷*1420*

[562] **5.6** Percentage increase in shipments of room air-conditioners each year in the USA ▷▷*628*

[563] **10** Years of oil left in the USA ▷▷*695* ▷▷*1411*

[564] **15.7** Tons of oil (or equivalent) required annually to support each American's lifestyle ◁◁*563* ▷▷*843* ▷▷*1311, 1312*

[565] **$1,321,100,000** Annual research-and-development budget of US military agencies for guided missiles ▷▷*843* ▷▷*912*

[566] **$353,000,000** Annual research-and-development budget of US federal government for energy conservation ▷▷*1145*

[567] **1.5** Average number of workers per US farm ▷▷*852* ▷▷*1110*

[568] **58,210** US farming families quitting farming on average each year since 1970 ▷▷*874*

[569] **14,204** Miles juggernaut loads of nitrogen plant food and fertiliser that is spread annually in the USA would stretch nose-to-tail ▷▷*1039, 1040*

[570] **14,226** Miles juggernauts would stretch nose-to-tail loaded with US annual production of meat and poultry ▷▷*1116, 1117* ▷▷*1213* ▷▷*1217*

[571] **13,134** Miles juggernauts would stretch nose-to-tail loaded with meat consumed each year in the European Community ▷▷*1060* ▷▷*1097*

[572] **923** Miles juggernauts would stretch nose-to-tail loaded with meat consumed each year in Japan ▷▷ *1105*

[573] **57** Football fields of pizza consumed each day in the USA ▷▷ *1064*

[574] **130** Plastic food-container units expected to be used per American in 1995 ▷▷ *1424*

[575] **1** Facilities for reprocessing used PET plastic bottles in the EC ▷▷ *1439*

[576] **2,147,000** Plastic drinks bottles thrown away each daylight hour in EC ▷▷ *1443*

[577] **54** Switzerlands of forest controlled by governments in Canada ▷▷ *1172*

[578] **75,000** Miles of new roads proposed for US roadless wilderness by the US Forest Service 1985–99 ▷▷ *1190*

[579] **13,818,589** Football fields of Canadian forest that burned in 1989 ▷▷ *1194*

[580] **1,040,723** Football fields of US forest lost every year ▷▷ *1218*

[581] **3** Switzerlands of US forest lost between 1970 and 1987 ▷▷ *1173*

[582] **464,992** Wild beaver pelts taken in Canada 1987–8 ▷▷ *1186*

[583] **91,414** Wild fox pelts taken in Canada 1987–8 ▷▷ *1183*

[584] **8,265** Wild lynx pelts taken in Canada 1988–9 ▷▷ *1185*

[585] **3,110** Wild wolf pelts taken in Canada 1987–8 ▷▷ *1179*

[586] **25** Kilograms of glass waste arising annually per West European ▷▷ *1222*

[587] **25** Kilograms of glass recycled each year per West German

[588] **5.6** Kilograms of glass recycled each year per Briton

[589] **£2,800,000** Annual cost of chauffeur-driven cars for Euro-MPs ◁◁*15* ▷▷*635, 636*

[590] **£0.45** Untaxed cost of pack of 20 cigarettes in the UK ◁◁*101*

[591] **£0.14** Untaxed cost of pack of 20 cigarettes in Greece

[592] **102,000,000** Cargo tonnage throughput at Port of Antwerp in 1990

[593] **150,000,000** Cargo tonnage throughput planned at Port of Antwerp in 2010 ◁◁*227*

[593a] **189** Number of air pollutants officially deemed hazardous by the US Environmental Protection Agency ▷▷*1429*

[594] **9.7** Infant mortality per 1,000 Americans born alive ▷▷*940, 941*

[595] **4.6** Infant mortality per 1,000 Japanese born alive

[596] **43,000** Cigarettes smoked every second in Europe, Scandinavia and the former Soviet Union ▷▷*605*

[597] **23,000,000** French people who wear glasses ▷▷*601*

[598] **1:100** Proportion of American men carrying the HIV virus ◁◁*391, 392* ▷▷*827*

[599] **7.9** Hospital beds per 1,000 people in USA in 1970

[600] **5** Hospital beds per 1,000 people in USA in 1988

[601] **250,000** People without health insurance in France

[602] **34,700,000** People without health insurance in USA

[603] **1,000,000** People without health insurance in Germany

[604] **10** A German's life-expectancy rank in the EC
◁◁*520, 521*   ▷▷*974*

[605] **23,000,000** Cigarettes manufactured in the EC each
working day ◁◁*101*

[606] **2.3** Doctors per 1,000 Americans

[607] **3.7** Doctors per 1,000 Spaniards

[608] **120** Soviet experimental nuclear explosions carried out in
the Volga Basin ▷▷*1297*

[609] **1,141,364** Native-peoples population of North American
reservations ▷▷*890*

[610] **£1,530** Spending on corporate research-and-
development annually per British employee ▷▷*912*

[611] **£4,320** Spending on corporate research-and-
development annually per German employee

[612] **300** Applications received each working day by the
European patent office ▷▷*750*

[613] **8** Times the number of ride-on lawn-mowers sold
annually would mow the state of Delaware in a day ◁◁*568*

[614] **1,900** Prescription drugs allowed in Norway
◁◁*308, 309*   ▷▷*615*

[615] **25,000** Prescription drugs allowed in the UK

[616] **11** Juggernauts required to carry the gold mined annually
in the USA ▷▷*855*

[617] **1,500,000** US lesbian mothers living with their children ◁◁*93, 94*

[618] **11,000** Number of times a typical US breast-fed baby's dioxins diet exceeds recommended daily ingestion ▷▷*709*

[619] **$591,780** UK mothers' daily spending on baby-care cosmetics and toiletries ◁◁*46* ▷▷*662*

[620] **$254,794** French mothers' daily spending on baby-care cosmetics and toiletries

[621] **10** Percentage reduction of annual nitrogen-oxide emissions per American 1970–88

[622] **39** Percentage reduction of nitrogen-oxide emissions per Japanese 1970–88

[623] **53** Nuclear reactors added to French national grid since 1977 ◁◁*274* ▷▷*1273*

[624] **2010** Date set by Sweden for shutting down all its nuclear reactors

[625] **430** Plans for nuclear-power plants cancelled or deferred indefinitely since 1972 in the USA ▷▷*1283*

[626] **7–20** Percentage of Russian crude oil spilt in pipeline ruptures ▷▷*1284, 1287*

[627] **170,000,000** CFC-cooled domestic fridges and fridge-freezers installed in EC, EFTA and East European states ▷▷*1351, 1352*

[628] **70** Factor by which chlorine in the European upper atmosphere exceeded normal levels in 1991–2 ▷▷*1357*

[629] **600** Lbs of product packaging discarded by average American per year ▷▷*1464, 1465*

[630] **3,802** Miles juggernauts loaded with Canada's annual newsprint production would stretch nose-to-tail ▷▷ *1487*

[631] **10,871** Miles juggernauts loaded with Canada's annual production of wood pulp would stretch nose-to-tail ◁◁*292*

[632] **270** Kilograms of waste paper annually per USA resident ▷▷*879*

[633] **$3.70** Annual expenditure on disposable paper nappies per Spanish female ▷▷ *1441*

[634] **$21** Annual expenditure on disposable paper nappies per British female ◁◁*46*

[635] **£22,367** Constituency allowance of German Federal MP ◁◁*49*

[636] **£10,138** Constituency allowance of British MP ▷▷*836*

[637] **165:1** Ratio of USA executives' average pay to average USA worker's pay ▷▷ *720*   ▷▷ *1450*

[638] **$49,752** Working day's pay of Mr Rand Araskog, head of ITT ▷▷ *1218*

[639] **$73,000,000** 1991 annual pay of Time Warner Inc chairman Steve Ross ◁◁*368*   ▷▷ *722*

[640] **19,007** Football fields of land with dangerous concentrations of pesticide DDT in former Soviet Union ▷▷ *1082*

[641] **14,000** Human deaths from pesticide poisoning annually in former Soviet Union

[642] **5,380** Miles of nose-to-tail juggernaut loads of pesticides sprayed each year in the USA ◁◁*568*

[643] **£2.50** Average price per gallon of premium petrol in France ▷▷*644*   ▷▷ *1310*

[644] **£0.73** Typical price per gallon of premium petrol in the USA ▷▷ *1209*

[645] **55** Kilograms of plastic waste annually per USA resident ◁◁*475*

[646] **17** Kilograms of plastic waste annually per West European

[647] **25** Kilograms of plastic waste annually per Japanese

[648] **14,000** Dead lakes in Sweden ◁◁*80*   ◁◁*155, 156* ▷▷*667, 668*

[649] **1.88** Percentage of US gross national product spent on pollution control

[650] **1.52** Percentage of German gross national product spent on pollution control

[651] **85.7** Kilograms of sulphur oxide emitted atmospherically per Canadian each year ▷▷*667*   ▷▷*1201, 1202*

[652] **877** Daily carloads of people added to EC population 1960–90 ▷▷*967*

[653] **22,385,640** US population increase since the election of President Reagan ▷▷*961*

[654] **2** Number of times US rail track lost 1977–87 would circle globe ▷▷*1251*

[655] **£81,500** Taxpayers' annual rail-service subsidy per route mile in Great Britain ◁◁*82, 83*

[656] **£439,900** Taxpayers' annual rail-service subsidy per route mile in Italy

[657] **£85,000** Taxpayers' annual rail-service subsidy per route mile in France

[658] **70–90** Percentage return rates achieved by US states making drinks bottles refundable ◁◁*107*

[659] **150** Kilometres of traffic tunnel which will girdle Paris by year 2000 ◁◁*542*

[660] **20** Percentage of the former Soviet Union's sewage dumped raw ◁◁*479*   ▷▷*1478*

[661] **26,500,000** Americans with less than secondary wastewater treatment ▷▷*1475*   ▷▷*1483*

[662] **60** Miles juggernauts would stretch loaded nose-to-tail with a year's worth of paper-based sanitary pads and tampons disposed of by EC women ◁◁*323*

[663] **333,458** Football fields the USA's 43,683 shopping malls would cover ▷▷*761*   ▷▷*1036*

[664] **15,000** Supertankers of topsoil that erode annually in the former Soviet Union ▷▷*1096*

[665] **111,587,000** Head of cattle on North American farms ▷▷*1143*   ▷▷*1213*

[666] **500,000** US sales of *Final Exit*, a $16.95 suicide manual ◁◁*407*   ◁◁*522, 523*

[667] **6.9** Kilograms of sulphur oxide emitted atmospherically per Japanese ◁◁*651*   ▷▷*1242*

[668] **198** Juggernauts required to carry sulphur dioxide belched annually from coal power station at Boxberg, (East) Germany ◁◁*518*   ▷▷*1384*

[669] **14,000** Items of TV sex viewed by US teenagers annually ▷▷*746*

[670] **1926** Date of the first all-electronic Japanese TV ▷▷*673*

[671] **10,500,000** British TV sets in 1960

[672] **2,000,000** West German TV sets in 1960

[673] **0.3** Video recorders per 100 persons in the former Soviet Union ◁◁*670*

[674] **28** Percentage of US households with more than one video cassette recorder

[675] **£59.44** Average per capita spending of five chief mainland EC states on overseas aid ▷▷*782*   ▷▷*788* ▷▷*801*

[676] **108** Visitors per minute to Notre Dame cathedral, Paris ◁◁*244*   ▷▷*813*

[677] **230,000,000** Mediterranean coastal population in summer

[678] **130,000,000** Mediterranean coastal population in winter ◁◁*244*

[679] **890,000,000** The Mediterranean's projected summer population by year 2075

[680] **55,000** Toxic substances under review by the US Environmental Protection Agency ◁◁*424*   ▷▷*818* ▷▷*1202*   ▷▷*1353*

[681] **31** Miles juggernauts loaded with a daylight hour's US generation of hazardous waste would stretch nose-to-tail ▷▷*1358*

[682] **1,124** Tonnes of poultry meat transported to the UK from Spain each year ◁◁*198, 199*

[683] **$14,500,000,000** Value of British manufacturers' exports to Germany per year

[684] **$21,800,000,000** Value of French manufacturers' exports to Germany per year

[685] **6.3** Motorway fatalities per 100,000,000 vehicle kilometres in UK ◁◁*303*　◁◁*551*　▷▷*696, 697*

[686] **9.1** Motorway fatalities per 100,000,000 vehicle kilometres in France

[687] **17** Road-tanker loads of petrol consumed each daylight second by EC vehicles ◁◁*550*　◁◁*626*

[688] **50** Percentage of world air travel that takes place in the USA ◁◁*244*　◁◁*286*　▷▷*892*

[689] **257** Factor by which car travel exceeds bus travel in the USA ▷▷*1302, 1303*

[690] **2** Number of US cities where more than one-third of workers use rapid transit to go to work

[691] **159,000,000,000** Increase in US truck kilometres travelled 1984–8 ◁◁*682*

[692] **15** Percentage increase in petroleum consumed by US transportation 1983–90 ▷▷*1254*

[693] **55** Percentage of urban passenger trips taken by public transport in central Europe ▷▷*1305*

[694] **491,000,000,000** Increase in US vehicle kilometres travelled 1984–8 ▷▷*1481, 1481A*

[695] **37** North America's percentage share of all cars, trucks and buses registered in the world ▷▷*1344, 1345*

[696] **1,500,000** Number of times French vehicles use British roads in a year

[697] **5,000,000** Number of times British vehicles use French roads in a year ▷▷*1342*

[698] **86** Airliners planned to be operated in 1995 by Sabena, operating 35 in 1989

[699] **2,000** European city pairs to be linked by hub-and-spoke Brussels air services by 1995 ▷▷*892*

[700] **0** Number of chemical, biological and nuclear weapons allowed Germany by its Treaty of Union ▷▷*911*

[701] **1** Russian nuclear submarine production per six weeks ◁◁*459* ▷▷*704*

[702] **£4,600,000,000** Annual post-Cold War cost of NATO ▷▷*1105*

[703] **14** Nuclear-powered nuclear-armed submarines owned by UK Ministry of Defence

[704] **0** Nuclear-powered nuclear-armed submarines owned by Spain's Ministry of Defence

[705] **21** Miles of nose-to-tail juggernaut loads of municipal waste generated by North Americans per daylight hour ▷▷*708* ▷▷*1427*

[706] **1,076** Miles juggernauts would stretch loaded nose-to-tail with fruit and vegetables destroyed by the European Commission in 1987 to protect prices ◁◁*526, 527*

[707] **35** Miles of nose-to-tail juggernaut loads of shaving products used up each day in the EC ▷▷*1105*

[708] **24–40** Percentage reduction in garbage achieved by US municipalities which charged collection by volume ▷▷*1431*

[709] **55** Supertankers of waste-incinerator ash requiring disposal each year in the USA ▷▷*1008*

[710] **38,600,000** Average annual income required to clean up US toxic waste sites ▷▷*782*

[711] **1,205** Miles juggernauts would stretch nose-to-tail loaded with excrement and urine from a year's dumped paper nappies in the USA ◁◁*29*

[712] **4,794** Tonnes of lavatory paper flushed down EC drains each day ▷▷ *1483*

[713] **102,272** Juggernaut loads of plastic bottles thrown away each year in the EC ▷▷ *1459*

[714] **186** Kilograms of household and commercial waste annually per person in Russia ▷▷ *1486*

[715] **15,000** Hazardous waste sites awaiting evaluation in former East German territory ◁◁*421*

[716] **1,454** Juggernaut loads of hazardous waste officially unaccounted for arising from Prague industry annually ◁◁*425*

[717] **64.9** Percentage of US women aged 15 –24 using contraceptive pills ▷▷*885*   ▷▷*926*

[718] **2,054** Divorces per working day in EC ◁◁*93, 94* ◁◁*485*

[719] **$4,000,000,000** Annual cost to US health insurers of women's genital (pelvic) inflammatory disease ◁◁*717*

[720] **21:1** Ratio of German executives' average pay to average German worker's pay ◁◁*637*

[721] **2** Percentage of news content of 1,000 US TV networks that deals with working-class concerns each year ◁◁*669*

[722] **$5,000,000,000** Estimated net worth of US media tycoon John Werner Kluge, owner of an 80,000 acre estate and castle in Scotland

[723] **£600,000,000** India's expenditure on UK-made fertilisers per year ▷▷ *735, 736* ▷▷ *873*

[724] **800,000** Sheep in Kuwait before 1991 Iraqi takeover ▷▷ *815* ▷▷ *1288*

[725] **10,000** Sheep in Kuwait after Operation Desert Storm ▷▷ *816*

[726] **$780,000,000,000** China's total military capital stock predicted for 2010 ▷▷ *1200*

[727] **$130,000,000,000** India's total military capital stock predicted for 2010 ▷▷ *1479*

[728] **554** People per car in India ▷▷ *1321*

[729] **1,374** People per car in China ▷▷ *753*

[730] **14,000,000** Children dying before their fifth birthday globally ▷▷ *827*

[731] **5.8** People sharing an average room in Lagos, Nigeria ▷▷ *945* ▷▷ *1001*

[732] **38** A Tanzanian's annual energy consumption in kilos (coal equivalent) ▷▷ *1027* ▷▷ *1150*

[733] **1,442** A Cuban's annual energy consumption in kilos (coal equivalent) ▷▷ *1028*

[734] **23** A Nepalese's annual energy consumption in kilos (coal equivalent) ▷▷ *1056*

[735] **4,500,000** Japan's annual production of commercial vehicles ▷▷ *1303*

[736] **170,000** India's annual production of commercial vehicles ▷▷ *885* ▷▷ *1040*

[737] **144,829** Post Offices in India ▷▷ *1067, 1068*

[738] **5** Percentage of homes with postal delivery in Turkey
▷▷*811* ▷▷*900*

[739] **80** Percentage of homes with postal delivery in Senegal
▷▷*812* ▷▷*1300*

[740] **100** Average users per telephone callbox in Switzerland
▷▷*811* ▷▷*900*

[741] **30,000** Average users per telephone callbox in India

[742] **11** Percentage of women of reproductive age in Pakistan
estimated to use some form of birth control ◁◁*730*

[743] **78** Percentage of women of reproductive age in Italy
estimated to use some form of birth control ▷▷*936*

[744] **2.0** Annual murders per 100,000 population in Toronto
▷▷*828*

[745] **38.7** Annual murders per 100,000 population in the
Philippines ▷▷*895*

[746] **75** Percentage adult-illiteracy rate in Saudi Arabia
▷▷*1252*

[747] **$0.10** Vietnam's average hourly factory wage ▷▷*814*

[748] **18** Percentage adult-illiteracy rate in Vietnam ◁◁*746*

[749] **854** Bookshops in South Africa

[750] **78,186** Bookshops in Japan

[751] **78,000** People evicted from their lands by the Volta dam,
Ghana ▷▷*765*

[752] **120,000** People evicted from their lands by the Aswan
dam, Egypt ▷▷*765*

[753] **1,000,000** People to be displaced by Three Gorges dam on China's Yangtse River ▷▷ *765*

[754] **10,000,000** Chinese relocated by water management projects since late 1950s

[755] **100,000** Rural poor and tribal peoples to be displaced by Sardar Darovar dam, Narmada Valley, India ▷▷ *1105*

[756] **25,000** Indonesian peasants flooded off farms by World Bank-funded Kedung Ombo dam ▷▷ *1231*

[757] **30,000** People to be displaced by World Bank-funded Icha dam, India ▷▷ *1037*

[758] **30,000** Nalmas Indians to be flooded off their lands by Mexico's San Juan Tetelcingo dam ▷▷ *897*

[759] **$1,000,000,000,000** Worldwide debt of developing nations ▷▷ *1153*

[760] **44** Percentage of the Philippines' national budget consumed by debt repayments ▷▷ *1156, 1157*

[761] **10,000,000** Refugees from environmental hazards or urban development worldwide ▷▷ *1293*

[762] **1,500,000** Estimated number of people to be forcibly resettled by current World Bank development projects ▷▷ *765*

[763] **163,000,000** Cases of potentially fatal diarrhoea in South-East Asian under-fives each year ▷▷ *1399*

[764] **65,000,000** Cases of potentially fatal diarrhoea in Middle Eastern under-fives each year ▷▷ *775, 776*

[765] **2,500** Dams built in India since the Second World War ◁◁ *761*

[766] **20,000,000** Estimated number of people displaced by Indian dams ◁◁ *761*

[767] **5.36** Energy consumption per Briton (tonne/carbon equivalent/year) ▷▷*844*

[768] **0.27** Energy consumption per Indian (tonne/carbon equivalent/year)

[769] **120,000** Kilocalories of energy per day used by industrialised city-dwellers ▷▷*873*

[770] **20,000** Kilocalories of energy per day used by pre-industrial farmers

[771] **1,074** Football fields of tropical forest felled in India per working day in 1980

[772] **10,965** Football fields of tropical forest felled in India per working day in 1990 ▷▷*824*

[773] **36,114,615** Football fields of India subject to flooding in 1960

[774] **112,000,000** Football fields of India subject to flooding in 1984

[775] **$49** Average annual health expenditure per South African ▷▷*889*

[776] **$920** NHS average annual expenditure per Briton

[777] **31/34** Percentage of men/women getting higher-education qualifications in the UK

[778] **42/49** Percentage of men/women getting higher-education qualifications in Canada

[779] **15** Percentage of Hungarian dwellings with central heating

[780] **1,000,000,000** Estimate of the world's illiterate by year 2000

[781] **6** The southern hemisphere's average per capita income as a percentage of that in the North ▷▷ *783*   ▷▷ *805, 806*

[782] **$345** Average per capita annual income of the world South's poorest countries (excluding India and China) ▷▷ *807, 808*

[783] **10** Percentage reduction in incomes in most of Latin America in the 1980s

[784] **2,800** The USA's research-and-development scientists and engineers per million population ▷▷ *1124*

[785] **53** Africa's research-and-development scientists and engineers per million population ▷▷ *1128*

[786] **$10** Annual military spending per person in China ◁◁ *726*   ▷▷ *839*

[787] **$1,098** Annual military spending per person in the USA

[788] **$311** Annual military spending per person in Canada ◁◁ *777, 778*

[789] **$170** Annual military spending per person in Cuba

[790] **$459** Annual military spending per person in the UK ◁◁ *777, 778*

[791] **$8** Annual military spending per person in Nigeria ▷▷ *945*

[792] **10,000** Navaho and Hopi native Americans being removed from the Big Mountain reservation in Arizona to make way for open-cast mines ◁◁ *761*

[793] **17,000,000** Estimated deaths per year from infectious and parasitic diseases in developing countries ▷▷ *959*

[794] **586** Nuclear reactors planned or operating in OECD and East European states ▷▷ *1237*

[795] **0.136** Kilos of petroleum used on an average day by a Pakistani ▷▷ *1254*

[796] **10.4** Kilos of petroleum used on an average day by a Canadian ▷▷ *1256, 1257*

[797] **60,000,000** Estimated world number of girls with no access to schooling

[798] **1:1.2** Ratio of male to female AIDS infection in Africa

[799] **15** Percentage chance of dying before 30 as a result of AIDS of a 20-year-old Central African woman in 2010

[800] **22.4** Percentage increase in world population since the election of Pope John Paul II ◁◁ *743*   ▷▷ *1091*

[801] **21** Percentage increase in the world's Roman Catholics since the election of Pope John Paul II ▷▷ *885*

[802] **1,200,000,000** People living in absolute poverty ▷▷ *1218*

[803] **200,000,000** Latin Americans living in poverty ◁◁ *783* ▷▷ *938*

[804] **630,000,000** Number of people living on less than $275 per person a year ◁◁ *781*   ▷▷ *1105*

[805] **$21,200** Purchasing power per person of Australia's gross national product ◁◁ *783*

[806] **$790** Purchasing power per person of Kenya's gross national product ▷▷ *1132*

[807] **$13,960** Purchasing power per person of France's gross national product

[808] **$880** Purchasing power per person of Bangladesh's gross national product

[809] **40** Percentage of Burma's exports which consist of teak-forest products

[810] **970,000** Thai families to be evicted from the land for the Khor Chor Kor forestry and pulp-mill project ▷▷*817*

[811] **135** People per telex machine in Luxembourg ▷▷*1300*

[812] **383,680** People per telex machine in Burma

[813] **3,600** Egyptian middle-income households that could be supported by one multinational tourist hotel in Cairo ◁◁*752*

[814] **$3,400,000,000** Annual expenditure by tourists in Saudi Arabia ▷▷*910*

[815] **970,369** Tonnes of bombs dropped on Germany by RAF in World War II

[816] **1,080,000** Tonnes of bombs dropped on Iraq and Kuwait by US coalition ◁◁*724, 725*

[817] **40** Estimated percentage of girl prostitutes under sixteen in Thailand ▷▷*928*

[818] **$24,000,000,000** Annual world market in agrochemicals
▷▷*873*

[819] **0.4** Low estimate of hectares of arable land required per
person by the northern hemisphere's agricultural system

[820] **0.15** Estimate of hectares of arable land available per
person by the year 2000

[821] **10** Minutes taken by UK astronaut Helen Sharman to
cross Africa ◁◁*577*   ▷▷*892*

[822] **1** Hours of cross-country running to the top of the
breathable sky ▷▷*1351*

[823] **19** Average hours taken by Japanese plant to build a car
▷▷*914*

[824] **500,000,000** World total of cars predicted by automotive
industry for the year 2025 ▷▷*1060*

[825] **900,000** Worldwide sales of Volkswagen Golf cars each
year

[826] **65,000,000** Years of the Cenozoic era, currently being
ended by humanity ▷▷*1196, 1197*

[827] **10,000,000** Children worldwide expected to have AIDS
by the year 2000

[828] **450,000,000** Population of the world's urban shanty
towns ▷▷*889*

[829] **40,000** Years between Earth's changes of axis towards
the sun

[830] **2** Depth in miles of ice in Antarctic sheet ▷▷*915*

[831] **8,000,000** Cubic miles of ice in the polar regions ▷▷*906*

[832] **1,000** Planets that might have life-forms sending radio
messages ▷▷*911*

[833] **2170** Date by which Mars could become fully habitable ◁◁*826*

[834] **50,000** Possible human population of Mars by the year 2115 ▷▷*930*

[835] **3,000** Recorded sightings of UFOs by military and civilian pilots ▷▷*1298*

[836] **1,000** Medium-to-large dams under way in the world ▷▷*1233*

[837] **861** Dams in place or projected by the Philippines authorities ◁◁*765*

[838] **5** Percentage of land area of Ghana covered by Volta dam reservoir ▷▷*1171*

[839] **15.6** Number of times Switzerland would fit into area of South-east Asia affected by Mekong River Basin dam project ◁◁*726*

[840] **73,000** Terawatt-hours of electricity that would be produced by damming all the world's rivers

[841] **285** Large dams in place

[842] **2,000** Tonnes weighed by largest earth-moving machine

[843] **720,000** Fuel efficiency in miles per gallon (equivalent) of a blackpoll warbler bird ▷▷*1369*

[844] **2,000** Emission (in lbs) of carbon dioxide preventable by installing a low-energy light-bulb ▷▷*906*

[845] **70** Number to be divided by percentage growth per year to calculate the years within which growth brings a doubling

[846] **1,937** Switzerlands of productive land on Earth ▷▷*896*

[847] **13** Years it would take to deplete the world's known petroleum reserves if all food were produced by North American methods ▷▷*873*

[848] **0.09** Hectares sufficing to provide 2,500 calories per day per person in the USA

[849] **0.045** Hectares sufficing to provide 2,500 calories per day per person in Japan

[850] **0.3** Hectares sufficing to provide 2,500 calories per day per person in India

[851] **70** Genetically altered organisms formally released into the world since 1984 ▷▷ *1057*

[852] **250–300** Releases of all genetically engineered organisms worldwide

[853] **$20,000,000,000** World market for synthetic pesticides ▷▷ *1080*

[854] **500** Species of insect, including major pests, which have developed resistance to chemical pesticides ▷▷ *1085*

[855] **38** Tonnes of gold contained in a cubic mile of sea-water

[856] **44,000** US Congress staff on Capitol Hill

[857] **3,000,000** High estimate of human years on Earth ◁◁ *826*

[858] **11,000** Moving parts of the body ▷▷ *960*

[859] **71** Percentage of the human body that is water ▷▷ *1105*

[860] **10,000** Odours distinguishable by the human nose ▷▷ *895*

[861] **100,000,000** People worldwide with potentially toxic mercury fillings in their teeth ▷▷ *1008*

[862] **23** Years spent asleep in 70-year human life

[863] **5** Number of times Spain would fit into the world's irrigated lands ▷▷ *1108*

[864] **835,000** Book titles (over 28–48 pages depending on overall length) published worldwide in 1987

[865] **10,000,000** Books (over 28–48 pages depending on overall length) printed worldwide between the years 1437 and 1900 ◁◁*810*

[866] **1:3** Proportion of cropland per capita lost since the Second World War ◁◁*820* ▷▷*868*

[867] **15** Percentage of the earth's land surface degraded by human activities ◁◁*842*

[868] **3.7** Acres of world arable land per person ◁◁*820* ◁◁*866*

[869] **8,219** Tonnes of crude oil discharged into world seas on average day ▷▷ *1287*

[870] **4,320** Tonnes of oil discharged into seas each working day by oil tankers ◁◁*824*

[871] **1,154** Olympic-sized swimming-pools of crude oil spilt at sea in disasters since 1975 ▷▷ *1287*

[872] **20,000** Supertanker loads of non-fuel minerals used by the world economy per year ▷▷ *1377, 1378*

[873] **6** Barrels of oil-equivalent energy needed to produce one tonne of nitrogenous fertiliser ◁◁*818*

[874] **1,500,000** Tonnes of nitrogenous fertiliser used annually in the UK ▷▷ *1041, 1042*

[875] **1/40,000th** The power of the Hiroshima atom bomb compared with combined subsequent nuclear tests ▷▷*911*

[876] **922,100,000,000** Known barrels of reserves of oil

[877] **450,000,000,000** Barrels of oil pumped into the biosphere ▷▷ *1302*

[878] **0.25** Thickness in millimetres the ozone layer would measure if it were brought down to the Earth's surface

[879] **550** Supertanker loads of waste paper dumped every day worldwide ◁◁ *712*

[880] **£44** Value of a tiger skin in Rajasthan, India, in the 1980s ▷▷ *1179*

[881] **440** Strains of pests resistant to insecticides in 1965

[882] **1/1,000,000,000th** Concentration of pesticide sevin that can uncoordinate the behaviour of a large school of fish ▷▷ *1082*

[883] **14,000** Workers killed annually in the former Soviet Union by pesticide poisoning ▷▷ *1080*

[884] **40** Percentage of the Earth's net photosynthetic energy on land that is directly or indirectly consumed by humanity ▷▷ *1255*　▷▷ *1302*

[885] **0** Birth-control pills allowed in Japan

[886] **308,750** Acreage of Europe's largest surviving virgin forest, in acid-rain-hit Poland ▷▷ *1194*

[887] **10,000,000** Chinese born in 1986

[888] **13,000,000** Indians born in 1986

[889] **630,000,000** Extremely poor people in the developing countries ◁◁ *224*

[890] **50,000,000** Tribal people who still live in the tropical rainforests ▷▷ *1298*

[891] **20,000** Low estimate of supertanker loads of oil discovered in May 1991 in the Colombian Amazon ◁◁ *869*

[892] **3,500,000** Tonnes of ozone-layer-destroying nitrogen oxides spewed into the stratosphere by jet airliners every year ▷▷ *1221*

[893] **900** Nuclear reactors on earth or at sea ▷▷ *1267* ▷▷ *1297*

[894] **3,381** Satellites launched since 1957 ◁◁*576*

[895] **377,000,000** Urban people worldwide without adequate sanitary facilities ▷▷ *1425*

[896] **240,000** Supertanker loads of soil eroded from the world's agricultural lands since industrialisation ▷▷ *1096*

[897] **5** Number of times a year's worth of world soil loss would stretch to the moon and back loaded in rail-freight cars

[898] **10,000** Estimated supertanker loads of African and Asian topsoil lost to the wind each year

[899] **6,669** Satellites and other items of machinery in space ▷▷ *1297*

[900] **454,000,000** Telephone numbers listed in world telephone books ▷▷*960*

[901] **1:4** Ratio of energy required to make a black-and-white television compared to a colour one ▷▷ *1243*

[902] **40** Percentage of biosphere's annual net primary production used by humanity

[903] **3,000,000** Tourists arriving at the world's frontiers on an average day ▷▷ *1221*

[904] **7.8** Percentage reduction in concentrations of lead in the Greenland icecap ▷▷ *1044*

[905] **120,000** Low reckoning of football fields of world tropical forests felled each working day ▷▷ *1362*

[906] **1,186,000** Tonnes of carbon dioxide emitted in the USA per year ▷▷ *1356*

[907] **144,000** Tonnes of carbon dioxide emitted in all Africa per year

[908] **20,000,000** Lives lost in the 130 wars since World War II ◁◁*455*   ◁◁*565*

[909] **0.3** Percentage of Brazil's budget spent on defence

[910] **23** Percentage of Saudi Arabia's budget spent on defence

[911] **1,800** Nuclear bombs exploded in over 50 world sites ▷▷ *1282*

[912] **1:3** Proportion of all scientists alive who work on military-related research and development ▷▷ *1301*

[913] **100,000,000** Estimated number of scientists employed in the world military establishment ▷▷ *1415*

[914] **44,000,000,000,000,000** BTUs of world energy conversion in 1925

[915] **345,000,000,000,000,000** BTUs of world energy conversion in the 1980s ◁◁*884*

[916] **450** BTUs given off per hour by a person sitting quietly

[917] **750,000** BTUs given off by standard family car going at 70 mph ▷▷ *1413*

[918] **1,000** Tons of waste produced worldwide every second ▷▷ *1493*

[919] **4,230** Tonnes of used plastic nets and lines dumped in the sea each working day by world fishermen ▷▷ *1164*

[920] **384** Whales, seals and dolphins estimated killed each working day by discarded nets and lines ▷▷ *1283*

[921] **500** Tonnes of McDonald's US waste saved each year by shortening drinking straws ▷▷ *1457, 1458*

[922] **244,000,000** Urban residents worldwide without clean water supplies ▷▷ *1475*

[923] **3** Percentage of world's water that is potentially drinkable (non-saline)

[924] **608,700,000** Olympic-sized swimming-pools of water required for world irrigation ▷▷ *1070, 1071*

[925] **43,480,000,000** Olympic-sized swimming-pools of rainwater falling annually on the earth ▷▷ *1120*

[926] **388,000** Number of the 4–6 million annual abortions in India that are carried out legally in regulated premises ▷▷*987*

[927] **35:100** High estimate of the proportion of pregnancies ending in abortion in Brazil and Bangladesh ▷▷*1013*

[928] **200,000** Women's lives lost annually through illegal abortion

[929] **7,000,000** Official estimate of abortions in the Soviet Union in 1987

[930] **25** Percentage of African population under 14 years of age ▷▷*940*

[931] **4** Jumbo-jet loads of Kenyans born every day

[932] **175,000,000** Population of Africa in 1940

[933] **877,000,000** Population of Africa expected by year 2000 ▷▷*1151*

[934] **11,000,000** Victims of Alzheimer's disease in the USA and Western Europe

[935] **1,218,000,000** Women required to be practising family planning by year 2025 in order to slow population growth to 10,000,000,000 by 2100 ▷▷*999*

[936] **38** Percentage drop in world births if women who wanted no more children had the choice

[937] **10** African states in which nine out of ten women have not heard of modern methods of contraception ▷▷*1012*

[938] **925,000,000** Estimated number of members of the Roman Catholic church, which forbids artificial birth control

[939] **0** Verses in the Bible recording the teachings of Jesus of Nazareth on birth control ◁◁*800* ◁◁*801*

[940] **6,000** Children dying every day worldwide for lack of basic immunisation ▷▷ *1009*

[941] **12,900,000** Children aged under five dying in developing countries annually ◁◁ *110*

[942] **284,000** Children aged under five dying in industrialised countries annually

[943] **3,978,779** Jumbo-jet loads of children in the world ◁◁ *827*

[944] **35** Percentage of world population that children constitute ◁◁ *763*

[945] **1:2** Proportion of Nigeria's population that children constitute

[946] **1,637** Kenyans born every day ▷▷ *1119*

[947] **40** Children fathered by Senegalese drummer Doudou ◁◁ *961*

[948] **20,000,000** Estimated number of women with mutilated genitals resulting from customary African and Middle Eastern practices

[949] **54,000** Population of ancient Babylon ◁◁ *769, 770*

[950] **600,000** Population of ancient Rome

[951] **40,000,000** Population of Bosnywash, USA north-eastern seaboard megacity

[952] **1:2** Proportion of world population that will live in cities by 2000

[953] **82** Cities of over 4,000,000 population by 2000 ▷▷ *1316*

[954] **50** Percentage of people in developing countries using modern contraceptives ◁◁ *938*

[955] **9** Percentage of people in developing countries using modern contraception in the early 1960s

[956] **10.8** Death rate per 1,000 population worldwide in 1980

[957] **9.5** Death rate per 1,000 population worldwide in 1990 ◁◁*930*

[958] **20,000,000** Preventable disease-related deaths worldwide each year ◁◁*763*

[959] **95** Percentage of world-health-research spending that is concentrated on solving problems that are most common in industrialised countries

[960] **200** Manhattan phone books required to print the information contained in a human DNA molecule ▷▷*1297*

[961] **114,000** World abortions per minute ▷▷*1013*

[962] **685** Women dying of septic abortions per day worldwide ◁◁*927*

[963] **45** Percentage of world's women of reproductive age currently using modern contraception ◁◁*939*

[964] **1,700,000,000** Women of reproductive age expected worldwide by 2025 ◁◁*938*

[965] **730,000,000** Women of reproductive age worldwide ◁◁*939*

[966] **$3,500,000,000** Annual family-planning aid to developing countries required to match industrial countries' protection ◁◁*947*

[967] **11,000,000,000** Predicted world population by 2075

[968] **402,000,000** Women of reproductive age worldwide not currently using modern contraception ◁◁*926, 927, 928*

[969] **4,000** Known diseases that arise from genetic defects
▷▷ *1057*

[970] **200** Factor by which an African woman is more likely to
die in childbirth than her European counterpart ◁◁*940*

[971] **30,000,000** Low estimate of HIV-positive people
expected worldwide by year 2000 ◁◁*827*

[972] **1:2** Proportion of HIV-positive residents in San
Francisco's population

[973] **82** Average life expectancy in Japan

[974] **48** Average life expectancy in Bhutan

[975] **4** Months' life expectancy is expected to increase
worldwide each year

[976] **65** Average world life expectancy

[977] **76** Average life expectancy in industrialised countries

[978] **50** Average life expectancy in poorest countries

[979] **62** Average life expectancy in developing countries

[980] **21,600,000** Combined population of Algeria and Morocco
in 1960

[981] **50,500,000** Combined population of Algeria and Morocco
in 1990

[982] **95,000,000** Combined population of Algeria and Morocco
predicted for 2025

[983] **11.6** Average age of marriage for girls in Bangladesh
◁◁*743*

[984] **15.7** Average age of marriage for girls in Sierra Leone,
West Africa

[985] **223** Persons per square kilometre in South Asia

[986] **14** Persons per square kilometre in North America

[987] **1,000,000** World population increase every four days
▷▷ *1003, 1004, 1005*

[988] **177** Estimated world population increase per minute

[989] **107.8** Percentage population increase officially predicted
for Central America 1975–2010

[990] **250,000** Addition to world's population per day ◁◁*800*
◁◁*801*

[991] **14,000,000,000** Predicted world population by year 2100
▷▷ *1051*

[992] **30.4** Percentage population increase officially predicted
for North America 1975–2010 ▷▷ *1251*

[993] **520,000,000** Carloads of extra people in South Asia
predicted by 2010 ▷▷ *1350*

[994] **120** Years of world population growth ahead ◁◁*895*

[995] **1,000,000** Carloads of extra people expected in Calcutta
by 2025 ▷▷ *1344*

[996] **1.8** World replacement rate of children per family in
industrially developed conditions and in ancient traditional
societies

[997] **1,000,000** Carloads of extra people expected in Europe
by year 2010

[998] **6** Number of times India's population will exceed the
USA's current population within next two generations
◁◁*769, 770*

[999] **42,500** Jumbo-jet loads of extra people expected in
Oceania by year 2010 ◁◁*962*

[1000] **909** Full Giants' Stadia of extra people expected in North America by year 2010 ◁◁*780*

[1001] **1,750,000** Jumbo-jet loads of extra people expected in Latin America by year 2010 ◁◁*938, 939*

[1002] **3,000,000** Years taken by humanity to reach a thousand million population

[1003] **100** Further years taken by humanity to reach two thousand million population

[1004] **30** Further years taken by humanity to reach three thousand million population

[1005] **15** Further years taken by humanity to reach four thousand million population

[1006] **25** Factor by which the resource consumption of a child born in a developed country will exceed that of one born in India ◁◁*933*

[1007] **50** Percentage reduction in men's average sperm count between 1940 and 1990 ◁◁*948*

[1008] **22–29** Pounds of mercury vapour estimated to be emitted annually by a typical crematorium chimney ◁◁*861*

[1009] **80** Percentage of world children reached by vaccination ◁◁*940*

[1010] **3,000** Villages in India with a family-planning service

[1011] **600,000** Villages in India

[1012] **21** Percentage of African girls enrolled in secondary education

[1013] **53** Percentage of girls enrolled in secondary education in Latin America ◁◁*938, 939*

[1014] **39** Percentage of Arab States' girls enrolled in secondary education ◁◁*995*

[1015] **33** Percentage of Asian States' girls enrolled in secondary education

[1016] **30** Percentage of world households headed by women

▶ ▶ RESOURCE CONTROL

[1017] **1,300,000,000** Head of cattle on Earth ▷▷ *1074* ▷▷ *1379*

[1018] **55** Square feet of rain forest that need clearing to produce enough beef for a quarter-pound hamburger ▷▷ *1072*

[1019] **16** Percentage of energy input to a 1 kg white breadloaf that is packaging and transportation ▷▷ *1222*

[1020] **0.350** Weekly kilos of bread consumed per American in 1990s

[1021] **0.765** Weekly kilos of bread consumed per Briton in 1990s

[1022] **1.8** Weekly kilos of bread consumed per British worker in 1930s

[1023] **55** Annual kilos of cereals consumed by average Briton in the 1990s

[1024] **110** Annual kilos of cereals consumed by average Briton in the 1900s

[1025] **26,000** Children dying of starvation every day worldwide ▷▷ *1218*

[1026] **524** Miles semi-trailer trucks would stretch nose-to-tail loaded with chocolate eaten by Americans every year ◁◁ *889*

[1027] **18,000** Energy (k/cal) required to prepare a kilo of instant coffee ▷▷ *1053*

[1028] **1,800** Energy (k/cal) required to prepare a kilo of fish fingers

[1029] **14** Supertanker cargoes of cookies eaten by US residents per year ◁◁ *803*

[1030] **288** Varieties of garden beans grown in the USA in 1903

[1031] **17** Varieties grown 80 years later ▷▷ *1055*

[1032] **$27,000,000,000** Annual bank-debt payments from developing countries to northern capitals ◁◁*760*

[1033] **$7.50** Annual spending per US resident on digestive remedies ◁◁*276*

[1034] **90** Percentage of Brazilian government's agricultural research devoted to export crops ◁◁*1027*

[1035] **400** Supertanker cargoes of excess manure generated by factory farming each year in the Netherlands ▷▷ *1059*

[1036] **2,308,000** Football fields of world farmland lost per year to housing, commerce, industry, water projects, lakes and highways ◁◁*849, 850*

[1037] **35,230** Football fields of UK farmland lost to development each year

[1038] **63** Average acres of a French farm ▷▷ *1098*

[1039] **9,636** Semi-trailer truckloads of industrial fertiliser used in India in 1960–61

[1040] **194,000** Semi-trailer truckloads of industrial fertiliser used in India in 1982–3

[1041] **500** Supertanker loads of fertiliser used in Western Europe in 1950

[1042] **1,000** Supertanker loads of fertiliser used in Western Europe in 1989

[1043] **4** Factor by which nitrogenous-fertiliser use multiplied between 1960 and 1981 in the USA

[1044] **$2,000,000,000** Value of Californian crops lost through pollution ▷▷ *1475*

[1045] **17** Low estimate of the percentage of Indian crop yield lost to pollution

[1046] **$4,900,000,000** Value of crops lost in the USA's Ohio River basin from pollution ▷▷ *1295*

[1047] **4,000** Additives commonly used in processed food ▷▷ *1141*

[1048] **54** Countries irradiating food or planning to ◁◁ *26*

[1049] **129** Miles semi-trailer trucks would stretch nose-to-tail loaded with Florida produce to be irradiated each year

[1050] **1:250** Proportion of US seafood eaters who will get sick after eating it ▷▷ *1147*

[1051] **5,560** Supertankers of extra grain required to feed the world's population in the year 2000 ◁◁ *849*

[1052] **121** Supertanker loads of commercial frozen foods sold in the USA every year ▷▷ *1354*

[1053] **3,000,000,000** People dependent on fuel wood who will live in areas where it is running short in 2000 ◁◁ *1027*

[1054] **90** Percentage of fungicides used in the USA that are considered capable of causing tumours ◁◁ *818*

[1055] **$25,000** Average annual income US Department of Agriculture proposes to spend per year on studying plant genomes ◁◁ *853*

[1056] **$15,000** Average annual income to be spent on the human genome project by the US Department of Energy from 1995 onwards ◁◁ *852*

[1057] **$200,000,000** Rice-genetics and molecular-biology research budget of Japanese government and industry

[1058] **386,000** Square miles of 'ghost' farmland exploited abroad by the food-import requirements of the UK's unsustainable population ◁◁*1036*

[1059] **15,000,000** Hectares of 'ghost' foreign farmland depended on by the Netherlands ▷▷*1160*

[1060] **600** Supertanker cargoes of global-warming methane gas emitted by the world's cattle every year ◁◁*1017*

[1061] **50,000,000** Egg-laying battery hens kept in restricted cages under electric light in the UK ▷▷*1210*

[1062] **65** Research programmes under way to breed herbicide tolerance into agricultural crops ▷▷*1429*

[1063] **60** Percentage of herbicides used in the USA considered capable of causing tumours ◁◁*904*

[1064] **1,400,000,000** People in countries with inadequate nutrition ▷▷*1097*

[1065] **4,000,000,000** People with more than adequate nutrition ◁◁*1033*

[1066] **$32.50** Average spending of each US man, woman and child on ice-cream each year ◁◁*783*

[1067] **1,300** Supertanker loads of food grain produced annually by India

[1068] **2,400** Supertanker loads of food grain required annually by India in 2020

[1069] **$427** Annual expenditure on infant formula (powdered milk) per baby born in the USA in 1990 ◁◁*968*

[1070] **40** Bushels of corn produced per acre by a Nebraska farmer without irrigation

[1071] **115** Bushels of corn produced per acre by a Nebraska farmer with irrigation ▷▷ *1311*

[1072] **20** High estimate of fossil-fuel calories required to produce one calorie of meat nutrition ▷▷ *1394*

[1073] **0.5** Maximum fossil-fuel calories required to produce one calorie of plant-food nutrition

[1074] **3** Kilos of meat eaten by average Japanese in 1955 ◁◁ *1017*

[1075] **11.3** Kilos of meat eaten by average Japanese, forecast for 1995

[1076] **500,000** Years taken for the water in the western USA's Ogallala aquifer to accumulate ▷▷ *1482*

[1077] **50** Years at current consumption before the western USA's Ogallala aquifer is depleted by agriculture ◁◁ *924*

[1078] **300** Miles semi-trailer trucks loaded with pesticides used each year by Third World countries would stretch nose-to-tail ◁◁ *818*

[1079] **3,000,000** Acute severe cases of pesticide poisonings each year, mostly in the Third World

[1080] **20,000** Unintentional deaths each year from pesticide poisonings

[1081] **39** Pesticides in common use in the UK that are banned in other countries ◁◁ *853*

[1082] **30** Percentage of insecticides used in the USA that are considered capable of causing tumours ◁◁ *1054*

[1083] **49** Pesticides in common use in the UK that are possible carcinogens ◁◁ *818*

[1084] **61** Pesticides in common use in the UK that are possible mutagens

[1085] **45,000** Different pesticide products on sale in the USA
◁◁*883*

[1086] **90** Pesticides in common use in the UK that are
possible allergens

[1087] **10** Percentage of food imported into the USA that
contains illegal levels of detectable pesticides ▷▷*1141*

[1088] **1:200** Proportion of cancers in USA thought to be
caused by pesticides ▷▷*1353*

[1089] **25,000,000** Developing-world farmworkers who suffer a
pesticide-use poisoning episode each year ▷▷*1153*

[1090] **1,081** Road-tanker loads of oil, phenols, detergents and
pesticides combined that are flushed into the
Mediterranean from France's Rhone river annually
▷▷*1283*

[1091] **$9,000,000** Annual cost of providing access to family
planning for 300,000,000 unprotected couples in the 1990s
◁◁*937*

[1092] **40** Percentage of all central American rain forests
cleared between 1960 and 1985 to make beef-cattle
pasture ◁◁*1017*   ▷▷*1394*

[1093] **12** Factor by which salmonella infection cases
multiplied in the UK between 1982 and 1988 ◁◁*1052*

[1094] **17.8** Gallons of soft drinks drunk by average American
in 1965

[1095] **45.9** Gallons of soft drinks drunk by average American
in 1989 ▷▷*1222*

[1096] **25,000** Supertanker loads of fertile topsoil swept away
each year by wind and water ◁◁*897*

[1097] **100** Jumbo-jet loads of people dying of starvation every
day worldwide ◁◁*802*

[1098] **70:100** Proportion of US cropland acres cultivated with price-supported crops under incentives that intensify land exploitation ◁◁*1034*

[1099] **1,000,000,000** Tons of world's largest crop, sugar cane, produced in 1987 ◁◁*1066*

[1100] **6** Heaped tablespoonfuls of refined sugar consumed per person per day in developed countries ◁◁*1026*

[1101] **25** Supertanker loads of tea produced by India each year ◁◁*1032*

[1102] **11** Supertanker loads of green and black tea exported by India each year ◁◁*773*

[1103] **10** Percentage of Sri Lankan tea exported in packaged form ▷▷ *1121*

[1104] **70** Percentage of available water in India that is polluted ▷▷ *1475*

[1105] **1,000,000,000** People worldwide lacking decent water supplies ▷▷ *1483*

[1106] **438,000** People in developing countries gaining access to safe water supplies each day during the 1980s ▷▷ *1505*

[1107] **1,000,000** Wells sunk in North China since the mid-1950s ▷▷ *1485*

[1108] **1,600,000** Tube wells sunk in India during the 1960s and 1970s ▷▷ *1205*

[1109] **200,000** High estimate of wells in the USA's High Plains region ◁◁*1070, 1071*

[1110] **9:100** Ratio of French agricultural workers to the rest of the workforce in France ◁◁*849, 850*

▶ ▶SUPPLY HOLD

[1111] **36** Percentage of arable land being cultivated in developing countries ▷▷ *1119*

[1112] **11** Percentage of the land surface of Earth suitable for agriculture ◁◁ *1080*

[1113] **16** Lbs of feed required per lb of beef produced ◁◁ *1072*

[1114] **250,000** Blue whales roaming the oceans in the pre-industrial era ◁◁ *1007*

[1115] **500** Blue whales left roaming the oceans ◁◁ *948*

[1116] **1,617** Calories of nutrition per person per day in Mozambique ◁◁ *1074*

[1117] **3,682** Calories of nutrition per person per day in the USA ◁◁ *1025*

[1118] **3** Number of US farmers per year who die from asphyxiation in manure pits ◁◁ *1060*

[1119] **179** Switzerlands of African land in the process of becoming useless for cultivation ◁◁ *931*

[1120] **1,074** Switzerlands of world land threatened by desertification ▷▷ *1372*

[1121] **1:5** Proportion of India's soil that is partially or wholly degraded by overgrazing, deforestation and faulty irrigation ▷▷ *1402*

[1122] **500** Members of the Indus River dolphin species left in existence ▷▷ *1433*

[1123] **650,000** High estimate of African elephant numbers ◁◁ *933*

[1124] **1** World ranking of Japan as an illicit trafficker in endangered wildlife species ▷▷ *1197*

[1125] **10** Reservations placed by Japan on endangered species it refuses to conserve ▷▷ *1423*

[1126] **30,000** Members in Japan's biggest environmental campaigning group, a wild-bird society ▷▷ *1242*

[1127] **50,000** Species lost in 25 years of replacing forests in western Ecuador with banana plantations ◁◁*890*

[1128] **101,000** Number of the 202,000 plant and animal species in Madagascar's 90-per-cent-destroyed eastern forest that are extinct ▷▷ *1363*

[1129] **78** Species of Australian native plant that are extinct ▷▷ *1403*

[1130] **16** Native mammal species rendered extinct in Australia's modern era ▷▷ *1154*

[1131] **80** Percentage of US poultry and livestock treated with animal drugs to promote growth or production or to fight illness ◁◁*1061*

[1132] **7:10** Proportion of Africans who are farmers ◁◁*821*

[1133] **1:2** Proportion of chemical fertiliser applied that never reaches crops ◁◁*1041, 1042*

[1134] **33.2** Kilograms of synthetic fertiliser used per hectare of Australian farmland

[1135] **95.8** Kilograms of synthetic fertiliser used per hectare of American farmland ◁◁*723*

[1136] **303.5** Kilograms of synthetic fertiliser used per hectare of UK farmland ◁◁*1022*

[1137] **360.5** Kilograms of synthetic fertiliser used per hectare of Japanese farmland ▷▷ *1363*

[1138] **2,000** Fin whales left roaming the oceans ◁◁*1122*

[1139] **30** Florida panthers remaining in Florida land reserves
◁◁*1049*

[1140] **1,200** Average miles travelled by an item of food before
it is consumed in the USA ◁◁*1048*

[1141] **34.3** Percentage profit increase of food producer/
packager Conagra Inc. in 1991 ◁◁*1052*

[1142] **21** Percentage increase in profits of UK food packager
and retailer Sainsbury in 1992 ◁◁*1047*

[1143] **$1,750,789** Pay of Chair/CEO of Chicago, USA, meat
packager Sara Lee Corporation ◁◁*1017*   ▷▷*1380*

[1144] **57** Percentage of US raw-log exports that went to Japan
until 1991 ▷▷*1194*   ▷▷*1456*

[1145] **0** Laws protecting endangered US forests ◁◁*905*
▷▷*1456*

[1146] **10,000** Miles of 'ghost' gillnet left floating in seas by
Japanese and other fishing fleets using 40-mile-long nets
◁◁*1122*

[1147] **70** Percentage of catch in a 40-mile gillnet likely to be
drowned dolphin ◁◁*869*   ◁◁*871*

[1148] **8** Percentage drop in world area planted with grain
since expansion stopped ◁◁*1006*

[1149] **4,000** Humpback whales left roaming the oceans
▷▷*1283*

[1150] **260,000,000** Africans not getting a healthy 2,360
calories of nutrition per day ◁◁*722*

[1151] **65** Number of countries considered by the United
Nations to be unable to support their populations in the year
2000 by current methods ◁◁*1026*

[1152] **200,000,000** Number of people who could be sustained by the food eaten by the world's rodents each year ◁◁*1051*

[1153] **3,714,285** Jumbo-jet loads of people worldwide suffering from malnutrition or seriously ill with diarrhoea, respiratory or other illnesses ◁◁*1100*

[1154] **144** Olympic-sized swimming-pools of ice-cream produced per year in Australia ◁◁*1025*

[1155] **5,865,000** Board feet of timber cut every hour of a weekday workshift in the USA's national forests ◁◁*905*

[1156] **146,000** Hectares of mangrove forest in the Philippines in 1980

[1157] **38,000** Hectares of mangrove forest in the Philippines today

[1158] **210** Supertanker loads of US meat, poultry and eggs produced in a year ◁◁*1074, 1075*

[1159] **1,450** Supertanker loads of grain and soy fed to US beef cattle, fowl and hogs in a year ◁◁*1017*

[1160] **618** Average number of gallons of milk a US dairy cow produced in 1950

[1161] **1,703** Average number of gallons of milk a US dairy cow produced in 1990 ◁◁*1066*

[1162] **425** Oil spills per month in the Great Lakes of North America ◁◁*869*

[1163] **1,726** New York Central Parks of old-growth forest left in six prime National Forests in the US Pacific North West ▷▷*1386*

[1164] **99** Percentage of the USA's Chesapeake Bay's pre-1870 oyster population that has been destroyed ◁◁*1050*

[1165] **0.1** Percentage of applied agricultural pesticides that reach target pests ◁◁*853*

[1166] **1:2** Proportion of pesticides used that could be cut by integrated pest-management techniques ◁◁*882*

[1167] **623** Miles semi-trailer trucks would stretch loaded nose-to-tail with one day's world production of pig iron ▷▷*1216*

[1168] **7,000** Estimated number of plants used by humans in history ▷▷*1183*

[1169] **75,000** Minimum number of edible plants available ◁◁*1030, 1031*

[1170] **17,391** Olympic-sized swimming-pools of timber exported each year by Indonesia ▷▷*1194*

[1171] **95** Percentage of rain forest destroyed in Nigeria ◁◁*821*

[1172] **75** Percentage of West Africa's forests destroyed ◁◁*931*

[1173] **1.4** Switzerlands of Australian rain forest cleared ◁◁*810*

[1174] **2,697** New York Central Parks of virgin rain forest scheduled to be cut annually in Indonesia ▷▷*1394*

[1175] **79** Estimated square miles of tropical rain forest destroyed daily in 1979

[1176] **150** Estimated square miles of tropical rain forest destroyed daily in 1990 ▷▷*1178*

[1177] **3,000** Varieties of edible fruit available in tropical rain forests ◁◁*1047*

[1178] **8,696** Olympic-sized swimming-pools of tropical timber imported by Japan each year ◁◁*809*

[1179] **$2,000** Top value of a kilo of rhinoceros horn in Taiwan
◁◁*1007*

[1180] **3.27** Supertanker loads of shellfish landed each year by
US states not conforming with federal sanitation guidelines
◁◁*1050*

[1181] **4,258,000** Acres of US coastal shellfish beds closed to
fishing in 1990 ▷▷*1483*

[1182] **80,000,000** Highest estimate of species on Earth
◁◁*960*

[1183] **5,000,000** Lowest estimate of species on Earth

[1184] **25** Percentage of species expected to become extinct in
the next 10 to 20 years ◁◁*1120*

[1185] **1:10** Proportion of world species' bodyweight that is
ants ◁◁*1080*

[1186] **1:4** Proportion of all plant and animal species known to
exist in the mid-1980s expected to be extinct in 23 years
◁◁*902*

[1187] **10,000** Sperm whales roaming the oceans ◁◁*1007*

[1188] **1,000,000** Sperm whales roaming the oceans in the
pre-industrial era

[1189] **6,000** Biologically threatened species in the USA
◁◁*1139*

[1190] **5.4** Percentage of heavily forested British Columbia,
Canada, protected from logging ▷▷*1455*   ▷▷*1487*

[1191] **417,391** Olympic-sized swimming-pools of fuel wood
lacking by 2000 ◁◁*877*

[1192] **7** Percentage of the world's land covered by tropical
forests ◁◁*892* ▷▷*1194*

[1193] **1** World ranking of Japan as a consumer of tropical
forests ◁◁*905*

[1194] **5,844** Olympic-sized swimming-pools that could be
filled by a year's imports of raw virgin tropical-forest logs
into Japan ◁◁*1144*

[1195] **12,012** Olympic-sized swimming-pools that could be
filled by one year's exports of Malaysian tropical hardwood
▷▷*1415*

[1196] **90** Percentage drop in western Atlantic ocean adult
bluefin tuna population since 1970 ◁◁*1147*

[1197] **94** Estimated percentage decline of the bluefin tuna
population due to Japanese overfishing ◁◁*920*

[1198] **1,200,000** Number of endangered hawksbill turtles
killed since 1970 ▷▷*1500*

[1199] **2,000,000** Sea-turtle skins and shells imported by
Japan since 1971 ▷▷*1146*

[1200] **60** Percentage of China's population with no access to
drinkable water ◁◁*830*

[1201] **20** Percentage of the world's fresh water that is
contained in the Great Lakes of North America ◁◁*1162*

[1202] **362** Toxic chemicals polluting the Great Lakes'
ecosystems ▷▷*1353*

[1203] **100** Percentage of the population with access to safe
drinking water in the former Soviet Union ▷▷*1271*

[1204] **28** Percentage of the population with access to safe
drinking water in formerly British Imperial Kenya
▷▷*1206*

[1205] **25** Percentage of the USA's Ogallala aquifer's original water expected to be depleted by 2020 ▷▷ *1213*

[1206] **400** Litres per day of water used per US resident ◁◁*1119*

[1207] **150** Litres per day of water used per French resident ◁◁*923*

[1208] **57** Percentage increase in demand for water in Canada 1972–86

[1209] **1** Olympic-sized swimming-pools of water used in the manufacture of five new cars ▷▷ *1345*

[1210] **40** US gallons of water used to factory-farm one egg ◁◁*1061*

[1211] **61,000** Olympic-sized swimming-pools of water per US resident used each day by US industry and mining ◁◁*841*

[1212] **7:1** Ratio of West Bank Israelis' per-capita water consumption to that of local Arabs ▷▷ *1504*

[1213] **2,500** US gallons of water needed to produce 1lb of meat ◁◁*1113*

[1214] **1:3** Proportion of California households using bottled water for drinking or cooking ▷▷ *1466*

[1215] **2,000** US gallons of water used to grow a pound of rice in California, USA ◁◁*924*

[1216] **35** US gallons of water used to produce one pound of steel ◁◁*1167*

[1217] **25** US gallons of water needed to produce 1lb of wheat ◁◁*1021, 1022*

[1218] **$3,298,192** Pay of retired vice-chair of US building and paper-product maker Georgia Pacific ◁◁*1163*

[1219] **217** Olympic-sized swimming-pools of timber extracted in Zaïre per year ◁◁*1172*

[1220] **2,173** Olympic-sized swimming pools of timber planned to be extracted in Zaïre annually by year 2020 ◁◁*1172*

[1221] **0.2** Miles-per-gallon performance of a Boeing 767 airliner on shorthaul service ◁◁*312* ◁◁*892* ▷▷*1369*

[1222] **3,750** BTUs of energy used to make one 12-ounce glass beer bottle

[1223] **200** BTUs of energy used on reusable glass beer bottle used 10 times ▷▷*1441*

[1224] **7,000** BTUs of energy used to make one 12-ounce aluminium can ▷▷*1416* ▷▷*1471*

[1225] **6,000** BTUs of energy used to make one 12-ounce steel can ▷▷*1435*

[1226] **105,000,000** Bicycles produced per year worldwide ▷▷*1344*

[1227] **540** Bicycles per car in China ▷▷*1349*

[1228] **8** Percentage of the world's people owning a car ▷▷*1396*

[1229] **36,240** Dams higher than 15 metres constructed between 1950 and 1986 ▷▷*1243*

[1230] **80,000** Dams in the USA ▷▷*1473*

[1231] **640** Kilometres of lake to be created by proposed Three Gorges dam scheme on China's Yangtse River ▷▷*1419*

[1232] **75** Major dams under construction worldwide ◁◁*842*

[1233] **83** Major dams planned worldwide ◁◁*844*

[1234] **1,500** Large dams constructed in India before 1986 ◁◁*766*

[1235] **530** Feet per year of siltation expected at Nizamsagar dam, Andhra Pradesh, India

[1236] **8,700** Actual feet per year of siltation at Nizamsagar dam, Andhra Pradesh, India ◁◁ *1229*

[1237] **52** Nuclear reactors exported by the USA ▷▷ *1445*

[1238] **9** Nuclear reactors exported by Canada and France each ▷▷ *1283*

[1239] **27** Nuclear reactors exported by the former Soviet Union ▷▷ *1445*

[1240] **51** The Canadian economy's percentage energy intensity

[1241] **25** The Italian economy's percentage energy intensity ◁◁ *843*

[1242] **22** The Japanese economy's percentage energy intensity ◁◁ *1198*

[1243] **5** Percentage of a typical desktop computer system's electricity consumption used by a notebook computer ◁◁ *843*

[1244] **35** Routine procedures that can cut energy consumption of electric motors by 50 per cent ▷▷ *1419*

[1245] **1,500,000,000** Square feet of US commercial space pledged to be relit with compact fluorescent lighting to save energy ▷▷ *1427*

[1246] **400** Medium and large electric-power plants that would not be needed by the year 2010 if 5 per cent of utility customers cut their energy use by 20 per cent annually ▷▷ *1496*

[1247] **10** Percentage of US gross national product spent on energy ◁◁ *784*

[1248] **5** Percentage of Japan's gross national product spent on energy ◁◁*1122*

[1249] **$2.53** Estimated social cost of a US gallon of motor fuel ▷▷ *1290*

[1250] **484,500** Olympic-sized swimming-pools of petroleum fuels used by the USA each year ◁◁*869*

[1251] **19** Supertankers of refined petroleum fuel used by US transportation every day ▷▷ *1255*   ▷▷ *1284*

[1252] **11** Supertankers of crude oil produced by Saudi Arabia per day ◁◁*871*

[1253] **2254** Year world gas will run out if four times current reserves are discovered and consumption is increased at its current rate ▷▷ *1369*

[1254] **9** Percentage increase in gasoline used in the USA since the 1973 OPEC energy crisis ◁◁*1139*

[1255] **$1,928,282** Annual pay of Chair/CEO of Texaco Inc. ◁◁*869*

[1256] **600** US gallons of gasoline per person used each year in the USA where gasoline is cheap ◁◁*824*

[1257] **150** US gallons of gasoline per person used each year in Italy where gasoline is most expensive ▷▷ *1400*

[1258] **8,500,000** Self-employed people working from home in 1985 in USA ▷▷ *1300*

[1259] **11,500,000** Self-employed people working from home in 1990 in USA ◁◁*811, 812*

[1260] **108** Olympic-sized swimming-pools of petroleum fuel used by US residences and commerces per day ◁◁*1053*

[1261] **2,000** Hydro-electric projects operating in the USA ▷▷ *1419*

[1262] **15,000** Private hydro-electric dams in the USA
◁◁*1028*

[1263] **328** Olympic-sized swimming-pools of petroleum fuel
used by US industry per day ▷▷ *1310*

[1264] **25** Percentage of world jet fuel consumed by military
forces ◁◁*892*

[1265] **25** Percentage of developed countries' electricity use
that goes to lighting ◁◁*1233*

[1266] **40,000** Iodine tablets held at each British nuclear-power
plant ◁◁*794*

[1267] **4** Brazilian nuclear-power plants built but not working
◁◁*890*

[1268] **438** Nuclear reactors under construction worldwide
▷▷ *1445*

[1269] **97** Nuclear reactors planned worldwide ▷▷ *1283*

[1270] **13** Giant nuclear reactors planned by Japan, generating
one-sixth of the current world reactor energy ◁◁*794*

[1271] **21** PWR reactor stations in construction or suspended
construction in the former Soviet Union ◁◁*1239*

[1272] **86** Miles semi-trailer trucks would stretch nose-to-tail
loaded with a year's uranium fuel required by the USA's
113 operative reactors ▷▷ *1308*   ▷▷ *1470*

[1273] **10,000** Years during which leakage must not occur in
high level nuclear waste dumps ▷▷ *1429*

[1274] **4,304** Miles semi-trailer trucks would stretch nose-to-tail
loaded with a year's Canadian production of radioactive
uranium mine tailings ▷▷ *1301*

[1275] **1,000** Supertanker loads of radioactive uranium mill tailings in New Mexico, USA ◁◁*906*

[1276] **100** Atmospheric nuclear-test explosions carried out in Nevada, USA, sending radiation fallout all over the continent ▷▷*1301*

[1277] **1,900** Atmospheric and underground nuclear-test explosions conducted worldwide since 16 July 1945 ◁◁*875*

[1278] **44** Atmospheric nuclear-test explosions conducted by France in Polynesia 1966–74 ▷▷*1445*

[1279] **22** Atmospheric nuclear-test explosions conducted by China 1964–88 in Sinkiang Province ◁◁*887*

[1280] **120** Atmospheric nuclear-test explosions carried out by the former Soviet Union in Kazakhstan ▷▷*1301*

[1281] **12** UK atmospheric nuclear-test explosions carried out in Australia ▷▷*1308*

[1282] **430,000** Estimated number of cancer fatalities added by nuclear-test explosions ▷▷*1315*

[1283] **46** Petabecquerels of nuclear waste dumped at 50 marine sites worldwide over the past 50 years ▷▷*1446*

[1284] **27,000** Oil tankers docking in UK ports annually ◁◁*869*

[1285] **2.6** Supertankers of crude oil produced by Canada per day ◁◁*871*

[1286] **3** Supertankers of crude oil produced by the UK per day ▷▷*1409*

[1287] **18** Olympic-sized swimming-pools of oil spilled on Alaska's coastline by Exxon Valdez supertanker in 1989 ▷▷*1377, 1378*

[1288] **193** Low estimate of Olympic-sized swimming-pools of oil spilt in the Persian Gulf during the 1991 war for Kuwait ▷▷ *1303*

[1289] **12,260** Tonnes of oil dumped into the North Sea from British drilling each year ◁◁*824*

[1290] **$1,812,807** Annual pay of Chair/CEO of Exxon corporation, owners of the Exxon Valdez ◁◁*440* ◁◁*869*   ◁◁*892*

[1291] **800** Pollution incidents believed to have been caused by the Nigerian oil industry ◁◁*1171*

[1292] **100,000** Low estimate of power stations in the world ◁◁*1246*

[1293] **20** Miles of road that average cars require for a typical trainload of 1,400 passengers ◁◁*1221*

[1294] **9,884** London Hyde Parks of deforestation in Brazil 1989–90 ◁◁*759*

[1295] **595,000** Miles of the USA's 3,500,000-mile complement of natural rivers which are dammed ◁◁*1105*

[1296] **9,000** Miles of US river under iron-clad protection from dams ▷▷ *1505*

[1297] **3** Nuclear-test explosions carried out in space by the USA ◁◁*899*

[1298] **100** Species that will be lost every day to the year 2020 at the current rate of world deforestation ◁◁*905*

[1299] **464** Average number of marine tanker casualties worldwide each year ◁◁*869*

[1300] **5,500,000** US company employees working from home in 1991 ◁◁*828*

[1301] **7,000** World sites of underground nuclear-test explosions where deadly radiation is stored ◁◁*726*

[1302] **608,573,000** Estimated world registration of cars, trucks, and buses ◁◁*876*

[1303] **3,055,500,000** Cars, trucks and buses in the world if rate of registration were at US levels ◁◁*870*

[1304] **836** Olympic-sized swimming-pools of petroleum fuel used each day by transportation in the USA ◁◁*1288*

[1305] **3** Public transport as a percentage of urban travel in the USA ◁◁*825*

[1306] **88** Public transport as a percentage of urban travel in the Former Soviet Union ◁◁*823*

[1307] **186,000** Jobs generated by a $3bn investment in rapid transit ▷▷*1402*

[1308] **160** Supertanker loads of radioactive uranium mine tailings arising in Namibia each year ◁◁*893*

[1309] **3.2** Number of times semi-trailer trucks loaded with the USA's radioactive mine tailings would stretch round the world nose-to-tail ◁◁*794*

[1310] **25** High estimate of gallons of water required to manufacture a US gallon of retail gasoline ▷▷*1333*

[1311] **18** Barrels per day produced by the average North American oil well in 1970

[1312] **12.7** Barrels per day produced by the average North American oil well in 1989 ◁◁*767, 768*

[1313] **88** Reactor plants built by Westinghouse, the West's biggest reactor maker ◁◁*901*

▶ ▶ CLIMATE CONTROL

[1314] **150,000,000** US residents breathing air considered unhealthy by the US Environmental Protection Agency ▷▷ *1345*

[1315] **1,000** Coal-fired power stations planned by Communist China ◁◁ *1246*

[1315a] **5,000,000** New smoking cancer cases expected worldwide from 2015 ◁◁ *1007*

[1316] **4** Percentage of Americans surveyed for the Motor Vehicle Manufacturers' Association who said they would buy an alternative-fuel vehicle as their next car ◁◁ *869*

[1317] **2,000** Square kilometres of Wordie Ice Shelf, Antarctica, in 1966 ◁◁ *773*

[1318] **700** Square kilometres of Wordie Ice Shelf, Antarctica, in 1989 ◁◁ *916, 917*

[1319] **2** Percentage decline in the volume of Arctic ice 1978–87 ◁◁ *1060*

[1320] **300,000,000** Bicycles in use in China ▷▷ *1414*

[1321] **45,000,000** Bicycles in use in India ▷▷ *1361*

[1322] **103,000,000** Bicycles in the USA ▷▷ *1400*

[1323] **20** Percentage of personal trips in Danish towns and cities that are made by bicycle ▷▷ *1377, 1378*

[1324] **2,400,000** Bicycle parking places in bike-and-ride transit schemes in Japan ▷▷ *1378*

[1325] **13,500** Kilometres of cycle path in the Netherlands ▷▷ *1414*

[1326] **1,500,000** Tons of Canadian air pollutants in the USA per year ▷▷ *1327*

[1327] **3,200,000** Tons of US air pollutants in Canada per year

[1328] **20,000** Supertanker loads of carbon deposited in the atmosphere by burning forests each year ◁◁*844*

[1329] **56,000** Supertanker loads of carbon deposited in the atmosphere by fossil-fuel burning each year ◁◁*906* ◁◁*907*

[1330] **20** Lbs of carbon-dioxide emissions saved by conserving a US gallon of gasoline ◁◁*1250*

[1331] **0** 1992 Earth Summit treaties agreeing to cut gas emissions by 60 per cent ◁◁*771*   ▷▷*1346*

[1332] **100** Supertanker loads reduction in worldwide carbon-dioxide gas emissions 1989–90 ◁◁*1263*

[1333] **2.4** Percentage of its carbon-dioxide emissions the UK could save by enforcing its current universal 70 mph (110 kph) traffic speed limit ◁◁*1251*

[1334] **8** Tons of global-warming carbon-dioxide gas absorbed per year by an acre of growing forest ◁◁*771*

[1335] **1:4** Estimated proportion of worldwide carbon-dioxide emissions from fossil-fuel combustion that was contributed by the USA in 1983 ◁◁*1155*

[1336] **280** Parts per million of atmospheric carbon dioxide in 1850

[1337] **353** Parts per million of atmospheric carbon dioxide now ▷▷*1346*

[1338] **460–560** Atmospheric carbon dioxide levels (ppmv) indicated by the year 2100 at current emissions ◁◁*1317*

[1339] **413,000,000** Tonnes of carbon dioxide emitted by US transport per year ◁◁*795, 796*

[1340] **19,000,000** Tonnes of carbon dioxide emitted by Chinese transport per year ◁◁*823*

[1341] **1:5** Estimated proportion of worldwide carbon-dioxide emissions from fossil-fuel combustion that was contributed by the USA in 1992 ◁◁*916, 917*

[1342] **3** Percentage of world carbon emissions from fossil fuels emitted by Africa ◁◁*906*

[1343] **26** Percentage increase in non-melanoma skin cancer predicted by 2000 ▷▷*1388*

[1344] **26** Number of days a year tourist paradise Las Vegas is dangerously polluted with deadly carbon monoxide ◁◁*1228*

[1345] **16.5** Number of days sunny San Diego, California, has dangerous levels of poisonous ozone in the air each year ◁◁*824*

[1346] **$492,957,678,600** Funds raised by taxing UN states' global-warming emissions at $100 a tonne ◁◁*914, 915*

[1347] **$80,746,356,000** 'Carbon credit' owed to low-emission Third World countries ◁◁*1342, 1343*

[1348] **44** Percentage of Americans surveyed who would not approve of limiting the number of large cars produced ◁◁*825*

[1349] **170** Cars sold per day by Ed Morse Chevrolet Inc, Lauderhill, Florida, USA ▷▷*1412*

[1350] **18,000** Miles driven by a car to consume a tree-century of oxygen at 30 miles per gallon ▷▷*1487*

[1351] **$2,137,000,000** Net annual profits of Imperial Chemical Industries of the UK, a leading maker of planet-wrecking CFCs ◁◁*878*

[1352] **$1,000,000,000** Dupont Corporation's projected expenditure on researching CFC substitutes over the next decade ◁◁*892*

[1353] **$1,403,000,000** Annual profits of E.I. Dupont de Nemours, makers of one-quarter of all the world's CFCs ▷▷*1485*

[1354] **10,818** Semi-trailer truckloads of CFC-11 emitted into the atmosphere in 1985 ◁◁*1052*

[1355] **68** Semi-trailer truckloads of CFC-113 used per year by US communications corporation AT&T

[1356] **6,272** Semi-trailer truckloads of CFC-113 emitted into the atmosphere in 1985

[1357] **18,700** Semi-trailer truckloads of CFC-12 emitted into the atmosphere in 1985

[1358] **$3,111** Working day's basic pay of the President of major CFC manufacturer Allied-Signal Inc. ◁◁*804*

[1359] **$135,000,000,000** Value of US capital equipment currently dependent on CFCs ◁◁*1244*

[1360] **1978** Year aerosols were banned in the USA as CFCs' effect on the upper-atmospheric ozone layer became known ◁◁*892*

[1361] **90,000,000** Low estimate of CFC-cooled air-conditioners in US cars ◁◁*824*

[1362] **10** Supertanker loads of ozone-layer destructive CFCs manufactured worldwide per year ◁◁*721*

[1363] **20,000,000** Throwaway chopsticks made in Japan from clearcut Malaysian forests each year ◁◁*1195*

[1364] **6** Years of serious drought in Southern Africa ◁◁*925*

[1365] **252,000,000** Acres of woods in Japan

[1366] **5,680,000** Acres of woods in the UK

[1367] **70** Percentage of the 3,000 plants, identified as having anti-cancer properties by the US National Cancer Institute, that are rain-forest species ◁◁*1018*   ▷▷*1394*

[1368] **$25,000,000** Annual turnover of Merck subsidiary Vegetex, selling glaucoma treatment Pilocarpine, harvested by helicopter from the leaves of the unique Amazonian jaborandi tree ◁◁*1175, 1176*

[1369] **26.5** Average miles-per-gallon performance of a new American car ◁◁*823*

[1370] **72** Average miles-per-gallon performance of a new Volvo LCP 2000 four-passenger car ▷▷*1409*

[1371] **50** Percentage of Americans surveyed who would not approve a 20 per cent per gallon increase in the price of gasoline for cleaner fuels ◁◁*1260*

[1372] **2** Degrees centigrade of climatic warming expected by year 2025 on current trends ◁◁*1007*

[1373] **$1,200,000,000** The USA's Global Change research program's requested annual budget for analysing global warming ◁◁*722*

[1374] **60:100** Proportion of world population not contributing to global warming ◁◁*803*

[1375] **1991** Year of death of Roger Revelle, early discoverer in the 1950s of global warming and the greenhouse effect ◁◁*1353*

[1376] **15** Percentage of Egypt's Nile Delta arable land that will be flooded by a three-foot rise in world sea levels ◁◁*773, 774*

[1377] **141** Total motor-vehicle production in South Korea in 1965

[1378] **1,321,630** Total motor-vehicle production in South Korea in 1990 ◁◁*1303*

[1379] **1.72** Atmospheric concentration of methane (ppmv) ◁◁*1092*

[1380] **0.8** Atmospheric concentration of methane (ppmv) in the pre-industrial era ◁◁*1187, 1188*

[1381] **$210,000** Grant awarded to Washington State University, USA, scientists for the study of cow-belching and its methane gas production ◁◁*1113*

[1382] **40** Percentage decrease in total ice-covered area of Mount Kenya 1963–87 ◁◁*1319*

[1383] **198** Supertanker loads of nitrogen oxides emitted by human activity in the USA per year ◁◁*892*

[1384] **1,550,000** Supertanker loads of nitrogen oxides emitted by human activity in Poland per year ◁◁*1347*

[1385] **£1** Cost per minute in an oxygen booth in Mexico City ◁◁*828*

[1386] **6,600** Kilograms of oxygen created during life of average century-old tree ◁◁*1350*

[1387] **1.07** Tons of oxygen per day released by the growth of a ton of wood in a forest ◁◁*1350*

[1388] **100,000** Persons predicted to be blinded by cataracts per one per cent decrease in total column ozone in the stratosphere ◁◁*892*

[1389] **3,000** Semi-trailer truckloads of carbon tetrachloride emitted into the upper atmosphere in 1985 ◁◁*1352*

[1390] **2,000,000** Tons of ozone-layer-destructive chlorine- and bromine-containing substances trapped in insulating foams, appliances, junked autos, firefighting equipment, etc. ◁◁*1351*

[1391] **20–50** Years a CFC molecule takes to reach Earth's protective upper-atmosphere ozone layer ◁◁*878*

[1392] **272** Semi-trailer truckloads of halons 1301/1211 emitted into the upper atmosphere in 1985

[1393] **21,454** Semi-trailer truckloads of methyl chloroform emitted into the upper atmosphere in 1985

[1394] **76** Square kilometres of rain forest that would have to be cleared daily to supply one day's US fast-food hamburgers made from Central American cattle ◁◁*1018*

[1395] **80** Percentage overall cut in US government budgets for developing renewable-energy sources from 1980–88 ◁◁*1255*

[1396] **11,000,000** Bangladeshis who will be displaced by a three-foot rise in world sea levels ◁◁*773*

[1397] **250** Supertanker load reduction in acid-rain-making sulphur-dioxide emissions by rich OECD countries 1970–90 ◁◁*1292*

[1398] **110** Supertanker load increase in acid-rain-making sulphur-dioxide in non-OECD countries 1970–90 ◁◁*886*

[1399] **900,000,000** Urban people worldwide exposed to unhealthy levels of sulphur dioxide ◁◁*1315*

[1400] **7** Hours of rush-hour traffic that are banned from downtown Rome ◁◁*824*

[1401] **3,000,000** Trees officially planted each year in the USA ◁◁*1190*

[1402] **100,000,000** Tree-planting target of US Global Releaf movement 1989–92 ◁◁*1386*

[1402a] **26** Lbs of carbon dioxide inhaled per year by a typical tree ◁◁*1336*

[1403] **1,000,000,000** Number of trees pledged to be planted in Australia before the year 2000 ◁◁*906*

[1404] **2,800,000,000** Estimated number of trees felled each year worldwide ▷▷*1455*

[1405] **4,180** New York Central Parks of US government forest that need reforesting ◁◁*1144*

[1406] **2,000,000** Trees planted in Kenya by Wanagri Mathai's Green Belt movement ▷▷*1487*

[1407] **50** Percentage of all broadleaf logs exported from rain forests which are purchased by Japanese business ◁◁*1363*

[1408] **1:73** Ratio of women to men among US automotive industry's top executives ◁◁*830*

[1409] **21,575** Motor vehicles produced in Japan in 1950

[1410] **13,486,796** Motor vehicles produced in Japan in 1990

[1411] **8,005,859** Motor vehicles produced in the USA in 1950

[1412] **9,888,036** Motor vehicles produced in the USA in 1990

[1413] **8,320,091** World total vehicle production in 1952

[1414] **44,165,033** World total vehicle production in 1990 ◁◁*1340, 1341, 1342*

[1415] **4** Days of global military spending it would take to finance a five-year action plan to protect the world's remaining tropical forests ◁◁*813*

[1416] **590** Supertanker loads of aluminium cans landfilled or littered in Japan every year ▷▷ *1499*

[1417] **200,000** Refrigerators, freezers and air-conditioners returned in Wisconsin, USA's Appliance Turn-In service ◁◁ *1244*

[1418] **$50** Reward for turning in a power-guzzling refrigerator to British Columbia, Canada, power utility ◁◁ *1240*

[1419] **7** Percentage of major appliances recovered after use in the USA ◁◁ *1362*

[1420] **10,000** Supertanker loads of coal burned per year in China ◁◁ *886*   ◁◁ *1315*

[1421] **4–7** Lbs of construction and demolition waste arising per person per day in semi-rural Vermont, USA ◁◁ *919*

[1422] **200** North American corporations with environment departments ◁◁ *892*

[1423] **40** Percentage of Japan's top 300 companies that have set up environment departments ◁◁ *1147*   ◁◁ *1196* ◁◁ *1363*

[1424] **30,000** Estimated tons of trash dumped in the Caribbean sea by cruise ships every year ▷▷ *1435*

[1425] **$6,473** Basic daily pay of boss of multinational detergent-empire Procter & Gamble ▷▷ *1482*

[1426] **14** Rank of Japanese in a UN study of 14 countries' state of environmental awareness and concern ◁◁ *1114* ◁◁ *1115*

[1427] **11,000** Pages of regulations drawn up by the USA's Environmental Protection Agency ◁◁ *869*   ▷▷ *1485*

[1428] **1,359** Waste sites posing 'serious' or 'some' risk to groundwater in the UK ▷▷ *1485*

[1429] **425,000** Hazardous waste sites in the USA ◁◁*904*

[1430] **10** Kilograms of waste generated per week by average household in Sheffield, England ▷▷*1458* ▷▷*1461*

[1431] **4** Number of times semi-trailer trucks loaded with a year's US household trash would stretch nose-to-tail round the globe ▷▷*1486*

[1432] **70** Percentage of municipal solid waste being incinerated by Germany and Japan ◁◁*879*

[1433] **667,000** Road-tanker loads of industrial effluent entering the Yamma River at Delhi ◁◁*772*

[1434] **2,500,000** Tons of coal equivalent that UK rubbish dumps could supply with their landfill gas ◁◁*1379*

[1435] **65** Supertanker loads of litter entering the sea per year ◁◁*1424*

[1436] **1,507** Tonnes of urban waste collected from the beaches of 25 countries in a day ◁◁*870*

[1437] **272** Tonnes of urban waste collected on 70 kilometres of Israeli beaches in a day ◁◁*920*

[1438] **23.5** Tonnes of urban waste collected from 20 miles of Venezuelan beaches in a day ◁◁*919*

[1439] **450,000** Plastic containers thrown into the world's seas every day ▷▷*1501*

[1440] **$27,767** Purchase cost per ton/day capacity of a US-made materials recovery machine for waste separation

[1441] **3,600** Tonnes per day of separated waste produced by city of Madrid, Spain

[1442] **50** Percentage loss of value of aluminium scrap in the USA 1991–2 ◁◁*1416*

[1443] **6,000** Tonnes of waste per day Mexico City can't collect
◁◁*1385*

[1444] **90** Percentage of surveyed Japanese who feel uneasy
about nuclear power ◁◁*1410*

[1445] **16** Commercial nuclear reactors being built in Japan
◁◁*1267*

[1446] **39** Commercial nuclear reactors operating in Japan
◁◁*1283*

[1447] **1.2** Lbs of waste paper generated by the average office
worker per day ◁◁*892*

[1448] **106,600** Road-tanker loads of oil entering the sea every
year ◁◁*1284*   ◁◁*1307*

[1449] **30** Tons per day of wet organic waste being composted
from 11,000 households in Toronto, Canada ◁◁*920*

[1450] **$5,539** Basic daily pay of boss of wasteful packaging
maker and forest exploiter International Paper ◁◁*1386*

[1451] **24,000** Miles semi-trailer trucks would stretch nose-to-
tail loaded with one year's packaging waste in the USA
◁◁*879*

[1452] **0** Tons of paper plates and cups recovered from
municipal waste stream in the USA each year ◁◁*1447*

[1453] **3,663,873** Tons of waste paper exported by the USA to
Asia-Pacific countries ◁◁*1363*

[1454] **1,218,000** Increase in tonnage of waste-paper exports
from the USA 1987–8 ◁◁*1190*

[1455] **5,096,000** Increase in tonnage of waste paper
consumed annually in the USA between 1988 and 1992
◁◁*1245*

[1456] **$4,250** Basic daily pay of George Weyerhauser, Chair/CEO of forest-wrecker Weyerhauser Company ◁◁*1145* ◁◁*1155*

[1457] **1.60** Lbs of paper and paperboard waste per person arising in the USA per day in 1988

[1458] **0.91** Lbs of paper and paperboard waste per person arising in the USA per day in 1960

[1459] **0** Tons of plastic plates and cups recovered from municipal waste stream in the USA each year ◁◁*1447*

[1460] **46** Supertanker loads of plastic plates and cups thrown out by Americans each year ◁◁*820*

[1461] **56** Miles of nose-to-tail semi-trailer truckloads of scrap plastic exported by the USA per year ◁◁*889*

[1462] **86** Percentage of trash found floating in the North Atlantic that is plastic ◁◁*1065*

[1463] **1.1** Percentage of plastic discarded that is recovered in the USA ◁◁*879*

[1464] **0.01** Lbs of plastic waste per person arising in the USA per day in 1966

[1465] **0.32** Lbs of plastic waste per person arising in the USA per day in 1988 ◁◁*821*

[1466] **17** Supertanker loads of plastic containers (non-soft-drink or milk) thrown out by Americans each year ▷▷*1485*

[1467] **172** Miles semi-trailer trucks loaded with plastic soft-drink bottles thrown away each year by Americans would stretch nose-to-tail ◁◁*1432*

[1468] **473** Miles semi-trailer trucks would stretch nose-to-tail loaded with waste plastic wraps thrown out by Americans each year ◁◁*1419*

[1469] **3,500,000** Motor vehicles worldwide running on propane gas ◁◁*869*

[1470] **1,018** Rail tank wagons of 'low-level' radioactive waste dumped every year in the USA ◁◁*1283*

[1471] **5** Canfuls of gasoline (or equivalent) saved by recycling 10 aluminium beer cans ◁◁*1224*

[1472] **40** Percentage of municipal solid waste being recycled by Japan ◁◁*1416*

[1473] **11,500,000,000** Kilowatt hours of electricity saved per year in the USA if all paper had 50 per cent recycled content ◁◁*1292*

[1474] **60** Factor by which pollutants in 200,000,000 tonnes of sewage pouring into 12 rivers of Shenyang, China, exceed state limits ◁◁*919*

[1475] **40** Percentage of Malaysia's rivers that are polluted ◁◁*1195*

[1476] **4,304** Miles of nose-to-tail semi-trailer truckloads of US scrap iron exported each year ◁◁*885*

[1477] **5.8** Percentage of ferrous metals generated in the USA that are recovered post-consumer ◁◁*1216*

[1478] **90** Percentage of Brazil's sewage discharged untreated

[1479] **209** Number of India's 3,119 towns and cities that have partial sewage treatment

[1480] **50** Percentage of the USA's 160,000 million gallons of solvents used per year that are recyclable ◁◁*1008*

[1481] **36.4** Percentage of rubber tyres recycled in the USA in 1960

[1481a] **4.8** Percentage of rubber tyres recycled in the USA in 1988 ◁◁*825*

[1482] **307,000** Gallons of water flushed by Arkansas River mouth every second ◁◁*895*

[1483] **55,000** Gallons of water flushed down US toilets every second ◁◁*1187*

[1484] **68** Square miles of New Jersey, USA, per toxic-waste dump ◁◁*1301*

[1485] **16** Supertanker loads of toxic releases injected into wells per year in the USA ◁◁*892*

[1486] **50,000** Trash trucks in the USA ▷▷*1500*

[1487] **75,000** Trees saved by recycling one Sunday edition of *The New York Times* ◁◁*1456*

[1488] **6,660,000** Road-tanker loads of untreated sewage entering the Yamma river at Delhi

[1489] **$2,987** Daily basic pay of Chair/CEO of dead-tyre-proliferators Goodyear ◁◁*1409*

[1490] **14,894,000** Landmines recovered in Poland since 1945 ◁◁*788, 789*

[1491] **25,000,000** Bombs and shells left unexploded after the Indochinese war ◁◁*908, 909*

[1492] **$97,000,000** Hourly world expenditure on military activity ◁◁*912, 913*

[1493] **172** Miles semi-trailer trucks would stretch nose-to-tail loaded with waste bags and sacks thrown out by Americans each year

[1494] **86** Miles semi-trailer trucks would stretch nose-to-tail loaded with clothes and footwear thrown out by Americans each year

[1495] **0** Tons of waste clothing and footwear recovered from municipal waste stream in the USA each year ◁◁*783* ◁◁*889*

[1496] **7.5** Percentage of all durable goods recycled per year in the USA ◁◁*721*

[1497] **0** Tons of waste furniture and furnishings recycled in the USA ◁◁*1053*

[1498] **1.5** Lbs of waste per person arising in Rome, Italy, per day

[1499] **2.2** Lbs of waste in 1987 resulting from an average Japanese

[1500] **3.0** Lbs of waste in 1990 resulting from an average Japanese

[1501] **4** Lbs of waste per person arising in the USA per day in 1988

[1502] **6.4** Lbs of waste per person arising in Los Angeles, USA, per day

[1503] **2.66** Lbs of waste per person arising in the USA, per day in 1960

[1504] **5** Average US households' annual consumption of water it would take to fill an Olympic-sized swimming-pool

[1505] **50** Typical gallons per day wasted by a leaky tap ◁◁*1105*

▶ ▶SOURCES & NOTES

References: the applicable year of the data may be provided in brackets ( ). Most information providers use electronic databases that no longer need datelines, being accessed instead by keywords and boolean searches.

Conversions: Tons = 2,240lbs in British contexts, 2,000 in US contexts. Tonnes = 1,000kg. A juggernaut = 22 tonnes/50 ft long (also 18-wheeler or semi-trailer truck). A road tanker = 30 tonnes/50 ft long. A supertanker load = 100,000 tonnes. An Olympic-sized swimming-pool = 2,300 cubic metres. A football field = 1.3 acres. New York Central Park = 750 acres. London's Hyde Park = 341 acres. Switzerland = 41, 293 sq km (15,943 sq miles). BTU = British Thermal Unit, a pre-joule Imperial measure: burning one cubic foot of natural gas releases about 1,000 BTU of heat.

Abbreviations: BAOR: British Army of the Rhine. CITES: Convention on International Trade in Endangered Species. CSO: UK Central Statistical Office. DRI: DRI Consultancy (London UK). DSS: UK Department of Social Security. DTI: UK Department of Trade & Industry. EPA: US Environmental Protection Agency. Eurostat: the EC's statistical office, based in Luxembourg. FAO: United Nations Food & Agriculture Organisation. HMSO: Her Majesty's Stationery Office (UK government publisher). IATA: International Air Travel Association. MAFF: UK Ministry of Agriculture, Food & Fisheries. MITI: Japan's Ministry of Trade. MORI: Market Opinion & Research International, London UK. NASA: US National Aeronautics & Space Administration. NHS: UK National Health Service. OECD: Organisation for Economic and Co-operative Development (Paris). OPCS: UK Office of Population and Censuses Surveys. RM: Rowland Morgan (indicating a conversion of the sourced number by the editor). UN: United Nations (New York, NY). UNCED: United Nations Conference on Environment & Development. UNEP: United Nations Environment Programme (Nairobi). UNFPA: United Nations Fund for Population Activities. WANA: Welsh Anti-Nuclear Association. WDM: World Development Movement. WHO: (United Nations) World Health Organisation.

UK ZONE [1] Advertising Association/RM. All advertising will have to show evidence of Product Life-Cycle Analysis and Green Auditing as the climate-forcing crisis bites. **[2]** RM/Dept of Education. Based on 1990–91 £18.1bn local authority spend and £3.5bn DES spend, 260 working days with 13.5 working weeks subtracted for holidays. Compare this figure with the daily TV advertising spend, remembering that education includes huge plant overheads. Actual 'knowledge advertising' expenditure in the school industry may well already be surpassed by the TV commercials that penetrate hearth and home. **[3]** Mind. A total of 5.5m. The population in old people's homes has soared over the last decade, however. Private nursing-home beds in Wales went from 1,168 in 1983 to 9,656 in 1991, an eight-fold increase. **[4]** MAFF. **[5]** MAFF. One acre in 1,214 is being farmed organically. UK total organic farming area is only three times larger than the Earl of Iveagh's farmed estate at Elvedon, Suffolk. Comparisons in the USA have shown that chemical farmers are no more productive than organic farmers. **[6]** Dept of the Environment. A total of 59,000 miles. **[7]** MAFF. One of the more astonishing phenomena of the European Community's agricultural plan is that a country which imports 46 per cent of its food and feedstuffs nevertheless pays farmers not to produce. It is known as the Set Aside scheme, and is considered environmentally friendly. Considerably more environmentally friendly would be to reduce Britain's average farm size to Germany's, thereby finding work for several hundred thousand unemployed. **[8]** MAFF. This expenditure is also, of course, a subsidy of food prices, and has a complex inter-relationship with Britain's huge 'ghost' acreage of agricultural production overseas, in tropical fruit, coffee, tea and tobacco, for example. Integration of unemployment insurance with farmer income could easily fund the restoration of Britain's lost peasant-farmer base, in order to de-urbanise some of the population. **[9]** RM/MAFF. **[10]** Giovanni Agnelli. **[11]** MAFF (1989), cited by Lang and Clutterbuck; *P Is For Pesticides* (1989). Sales of pesticides to overseas in 1989 are given as £655.5m. **[12]** RM/Dept of the Environment (1989)/Automobile Association. **[13]** Dept of the Environment (1993/94). **[14]** Dept of the Environment (1993/94). **[15]** Dept of the Environment (1992–3). **[16]** Elkington and Hailes, *The Green Consumer Guide*. Figures for all drinks cans are 3.1bn, alcoholic; 3.94bn, soft drinks. Weight of a can has gone down by 10 per cent since 1980. A total of 3,900m aluminium cans are used per year (increasing), 11 per cent are recycled, leaving 3,512m being dumped; 10m a day makes a stack about 150 times higher than Mt Everest. A 50 per cent recycling goal is set for 1995. **[17]** MAFF. Dead by end of quarantine: 379. **[18]** *Marketing*. **[19]** MAFF/RM. **[20]** MAFF. The continuing spread of mad cow disease is causing farmers to confront the necessity of slaughtering the entire stock. Breeding from affected cows' daughters is controversial in the National Farmers Union and the Ministry. The milk-drinking and cow-eating public is not kept well-informed. Methane from livestock guts contributes to global warming gases. **[21]** Dept of Agriculture (1990). **[22]** RM/MAFF. 1,750,000 tons of grisly cargo used until recently for animal food that may have passed on mad cow disease. **[23]** MAFF. **[24]** Turkey Marketing Council. **[25]** Science in Parliament (1990). **[26]** Home Office (1990). **[27]** *The Independent*. **[28]** Scottish Office. **[29]** RSPCA. **[30]** HM Treasury (1992 pro rata 1989). Palace spokesmen are keen to point out that more is spent by the taxpayer on the head of state's horses and carriages than on her cars (£84,000 in 1992, pro rata 1989). **[31]** MAFF. **[32]** MAFF (1990). **[33]** Surrey Wildlife Trust (estimated from a five-year survey of 30-mile stretch of Surrey A-roads). **[34]** Compassion in World Farming. A dairy cow lives out only a third of her natural life before slaughter. **[35]** Bank of England. **[36]** Bank of England. Japanese assets are nearly twice those of the US banks (1992). **[37]** Equivalent kilos of energy per capita per year. **[38]** RM/*The Economist*/Social Trends. For convenience, this calculation has Britons consuming 3,000 tons of coal-equivalent energy per year per capita, a rough average 1976–87 (*The Economist*), or 47 times more than a Bangladeshi. In other words, the environment can afford 47 more Bangladeshis than Britons per human birth. **[39]** Dept of the Environment (1991). **[40]** Dept of the Environment (1991). **[41]** Social and Community Planning Research (1990). **[42]** Treasury/RM (1990). Every man, woman and child. **[43]** Bank of England. **[44]** *The Grocer*. It has been known in African country villages for dogs to lick babies' bottoms clean. **[45]** *7 Days*. Bleached fibres tend to contain dioxins and other undesirable chlorine compounds. **[46]** Disposable Nappy Association/Pampers (1991). **[47]** J. Robbins, *Diet For A New America*. **[48]** MAFF. The Women's Environmental Network claims Birmingham residents have been shown to have dioxin body concentrations seven times greater than people tested in Thailand, and to be at levels which risk pre-birth damage to babies. This is denied by a government Food Surveillance report, which nevertheless says further surveillance is needed in areas of known dioxin emissions. The trouble is: EC limits are arbitrary – and poisons have completely differing effects on different species. **[49]** RM/Speaker of the House of Commons. Pay, travel and subsidies of MPs and their assistants each year come to £57,214,000 – and the British taxation system that they are directly responsible for is a shambles, with one officer per 900 taxpayers, a tiny fraction of the caseload of a family doctor; no self-reporting and direct rebate; and a self-employment scheme geared only to growth. The Short Fund by which taxpayers subsidise opposition parties acts as a strong inhibitor to new parties entering the House, because it finances the campaigns of incumbents, etc. **[50]** *The Economist*. **[51]** *The Independent* (May 1992). Olympia & York's badly-located extravaganza went bankrupt in May 1992. The monster tower, totally at odds with the rest of London's architecture, will remain as a symbol of the 1980s boom era, and a lesson in how to break every rule of good, convivial human city planning put forward by authors such as Jane Jacobs and Lewis Mumford. **[52]** Dept of Social Services. **[53]** Dept of Social Services. **[54]** DSS. This may be relatively efficient (at 14 per cent), compared with Canada, where critics claim government benefits are costing as much to administer as they deliver in payments. **[55]** DSS **[56]** RM/DSS. **[57]** Simon Wolff, *New Scientist*, 29 June 1992. **[58]** Dept of Transport (1989). Holland has 30,000 kms of single-use cycle path. How much has your area? **[59]** DTI (1991). **[60]** Press Association (1991). **[61]** *GQ*/RM. Only three property developers were among them. Top scorer was Alan Sugar (£3,075,962), boss of Amstrad, which marketed the PC3286 machine on which this book was prepared. His average £11,830 remuneration per working day would have bought 10 of the machines. Amstrad's fortunes have subsequently fallen off sharply. **[62]** British Plastics Federation (1990). A total of 510,000 tons, increasing each year, particularly in thin-walled containers, such as bottles (predicted growth of one-fifth a year to 1995) and in rigid containers for packaging food for household microwave ovens. Most of it goes to landfill sites, where it takes an estimated 500 years to decompose. **[63]** *The Grocer*. **[64]** Lang and Clutterbuck, *P Is For Pesticides* (1989). Of non-wholemeal bread, 30 per cent contained residues; of white sliced, 17 per cent, in Ministry of Agriculture tests, the authors report. Tests on wheatgerm in 1988/9 found 72 per cent of samples to contain residues of similar pesticides. **[65]** Dept of Energy. **[66]** Dept of Energy. It seems nonsensical, even insane, to spend seven times as much studying how to generate electricity in mega-projects as studying how to reduce electricity consumption. **[67]** MAFF. A total of 3,800 tonnes, or 33.4m ¼-lb packs: 1.14 kilograms per British cow. **[68]** Euromonitor/RM (1989). **[69]** Euromonitor/RM (1989). Nearly all households in Canada are served with 10–60 channels. Millions in the USA have cable TV, with up to 60 channels, including C-Span, devoted to politics, and Discovery, devoted to the environment. Why do Britons insist their TV service is so outstanding, when it is so limited? Regulators argue that channels must be limited to protect high programme investment. Why must programme investment be so high? Might not reduced programme costs aid independent, decentralised theatre, cinema and publishing? **[70]** Dept of Transport (1990–91). Britain's Secretary of State for Transport argued in 1992 that building roads was environmentally friendly. In the 1960s, the Conservative Party's Minister of Transport was Mr E. Marples, a road builder, who put forward roughly the same point of view. **[71]** Dept of Transport. **[72]** Dept of Transport. **[73]** CSO. **[74]** CSO. **[75]** Dept of Transport. Ranging up to 1.75m. **[76]** *Media Register*. Over £1m per working day to promote dangerous, neighbourhood-wrecking, planet-killer vehicles. What began as a luxury is becoming an expensive necessity. A government controlled by the road/motor lobby is paralysed in the face of a desperate national crisis as cities stifle, business slows down, small and rural commerce is destroyed, and oil wells empty. Advertising bosses Saatchi & Saatchi pay themselves £1,500 basic per day as their propaganda outfit loses £212,000 per day. Dealer adverts, etc., not included. **[77]** *Campaign.* **[78]** BBC/Dept of Transport. Most dangerous age for girls: 12. Most dangerous age for boys: 7. **[79]** *Planet Drum.* The US magazine says 6,600kg of oxygen are created by an average century-old tree during its life. A typical car at 30 miles per gallon takes 18,000 miles to consume a tree-century of oxygen. UK cars, working together, could consume nearly 13m tree-centuries of oxygen a year. And that's not counting other vehicles, industry or power stations. **[80]** Powergen advertisement (1990 prediction). **[81]** *The Economist.* Nissan's production cancels out Italy's quota of 2,000 cars allowed to be imported from Japan. **[82]** OECD. **[83]** OECD. **[84]** OECD. **[85]** OECD. **[86]** M. Walsh *et al.*, *Save The Earth.* A total of 6,500 gallons. **[87]** National Road Traffic Forecasts GB. Royal Mail vehicles travel 460m miles a year – a good argument for subsidies of facsimile use. **[88]** National Road Traffic Forecasts, GB. **[89]** Home Office (1989). *Culturelles* magazine says juveniles form 21 per cent of all offenders. **[90]** Health Education Authority/RM (based on 1990). **[91]** Dept of Transport (1989). **[92]** Church of England Synod. **[93]** CSO. (See 383.) **[94]** CSO. **[95]** Dept of Education. **[96]** *The Lancet.* **[97]** *The Lancet.* **[98]** DSS. **[99]** DSS. **[100]** OPCS. **[101]** Euromonitor. They'd stretch well over 4.5m miles – further than planet Pluto. **[102]** Euromonitor/RM (331m). Each British man, woman and child accounts for 1,682 cigarettes a year per capita. **[103]** John Button, *Green Magazine* (June 1992). **[104]** Dept of the Environment (1989). **[105]** Dept of the Environment (1989). **[106]** British Plastics Federation. A total of 19,200 tons (1992 forecast). Japanese manufacturers shipped 2,309,000 personal-computer units in 1991/2 (*Independent On Sunday*). None were known to have recycled or recyclable casings. Even if downgraded into things like artificial wood, most plastics remain non-biodegradable. **[107]** British Plastics Federation (1990). Blow moulding, mostly of containers for products such as washing-up liquid and milk, uses 42 per cent of UK consumption of 380,000 tons of HDP per year (586 miles of nose-to-tail juggernauts). The industry admits that the 'green' practice of using film refill pouches appears so far to have had little effect on the awesome numbers of plastic bottles, tubs and jugs being distributed, most of which go into landfills or litter. **[108]** CSO (1991). **[109]** Harry Cohen, MP. **[110]** Harry Cohen, MP. **[111]** National Association of Probation Officers. **[112]** Harry Cohen, MP. **[113]** Harry Cohen, MP. **[114]** Home Office. **[115]** Home Office. **[116]** Home Office (1992). **[117]** *The Spectator.* **[118]** *The Spectator.* **[119]** Performing Rights Society (1990). **[120]** Public Lending Right. **[121]** Guinness. **[122]** *Studio* magazine, (1990). **[123]** Guinness. **[124]** Guinness (1990). **[125]** RM/Ministry of Agriculture, Fisheries and Food/Hansard Written Parliamentary Answers. **[126]** Frank Dobson, MP. **[127]** Frank Dobson, MP.

[128] Ministry of Defence (1990–91). [129] Office of Arts and Libraries (1990–91). [130] MORI, *Typically British?* (1991). [131] MORI, *Typically British?* (1991). [132] *New Statesman & Society*. [133] Office of Arts and Libraries (1990–91). [134] DTI. Hundreds of thousands are imported from neighbouring Thailand. [135] DTI. [136] Dept of Transport. Kilos of carbon dioxide/km emitted per person on 5–50km trips of the sort crossing the Severn reach 0.96 for one-up cars, 0.80 for motor cycles, negligible amounts for bicycles. Perhaps a cycle-transporting shuttle bus can be laid on. [137] *New Consumer*. [138] Dept of Transport (1990). [139] RM/Cycle Campaigners. Bicycles produce negligible global-warming gases and no other pollution in operation, yet their share of roads in polluted and congested London is unmeasurably small. Some estimators thought this figure might be too generous. Holland has 30,000km of segregated cycle paths which connect real destinations. [140] *Construction News*. [141]RM/*Sunday Times*/CSO. By 1992, property prices were facing collapse, along with the major banks that relied on them. Since 1960, bank loans multiplied by 2,823 times. [142] CSO. [143] RM/Ministry of Defence. The Ministry occupies 1,363 sq. m, or 872,320 acres. [144] Ministry of Overseas Development. [145] Ministry of Defence. The ministry admitted £355,500,000 was spent on its computers 1986–90, in a 1990 Parliamentary Written Answer. [146] Civil Service. In years to come, this situation will be compared for negligence with the medieval inability to trace the plague to rats. Pesticides all have different effects on different species. Many were developed from chemical weapons made during World War II and have never been tested on anyone for an average lifetime. Britain's farms, and its food supply, are an open laboratory with consumers being the chemical companies' guinea pigs. [147] Civil Service. [148] Eurostat. [149] Eurostat. Most Britons would consider Spain a backward country, but it provides its people with twice as many doctors as the UK. [150] Release/RM (1991). At street level, police now find cannabis laws unenforceable, and liable to bring the police into disrepute. Merseyside police now caution users. Even judges are now recognising that drug prohibition is a stupid policy, which hands tax-free fortunes to criminals. [151] Treasury/RM (44,430,000 imp. gallons). Loaded in road tankers nose-to-tail, daily whisky production would stretch 631 miles. Imagine what this fountain of intoxication looks like to those Islamic countries with over 400m population where alcoholic intoxicants are hardly known! [152] MAFF (1990). [153] Lord Harris of High Cross (non-teaching staff central and local). [154] Lord Harris of High Cross. [155] CSO. [156] CSO. [157] Dept of Energy (1989). [158] *Liberation*. [159] *Liberation*. Hydro-electric power is essentially solar power, but dams have many drawbacks, among them their impact on wildlife ecology, river flow and long-term siltation. [160] Heinemann Philip. [161] Heinemann Philip. [162] Dept of Energy. [163] Dept of the Environment. Disposing of nuclear waste has been compared

to inventing a parachute after you have jumped out of the plane. It is wrong to burden thousands of future generations with the dangers of radiation from twentieth-century waste. **[164]** Dept of Employment (plants where off-site emergency plan is required). **[165]** Dept of Energy. **[166]** Dept of Energy. **[167]** Dept of Energy. **[168]** MAFF/RM. Millions of the able-bodied unemployed could be returned to the land under Britain's unemployment insurance scheme, thereby reducing the size of farms, intensifying labour and reducing dependence on chemicals. **[169]** Welsh Office (1991). **[170]** MAFF (1992 extrapolated from 1990). **[171]** MAFF (1990). Well over half this amount is given to Welsh hill farmers by the taxpayer. **[172]** MAFF. **[173]** MAFF. **[174]** *Book of World Rankings.* **[175]** *Book of World Rankings.* **[176]** OPCS. **[177]** MAFF/RM. **[178]** RM/Dept of Agriculture. A total of 56,000 tons. Parsnips are still a favoured vegetable in such areas as north-eastern Scotland, but it still seems strange that over £18m a year is spent paying farmers not to produce, when those that do produce, produce so many parsnips. Turnips sell for 20 pence each wrapped in cling film at Marks & Spencers 'speciality' food stores. **[179]** *The Grocer.* (1990: £11,700,000,000.) **[180]** Dept of Agriculture. The set aside scheme has an environmentally friendly component, but it is nonsense when hundreds of thousands of families need returning from cities to the land. **[181]** Lord President of the Council (1990). Free-range eggs constitute two per cent of the eggs sold. Nearly all hens live half-lives in electrically-lit concentration camps. US environmentalist Jeremy Rifkin warns that genetically engineered hens are on the way, which will have no legs, wings or heads, and will be drip-fed. **[182]** MAFF. Fatty foods such as beef, lamb and pork put humans at the top of the food chain, receiving the highest concentrations of pesticide and other poison residues. **[183]** MAFF (Autumn 1991). The National Farmers Union is struggling with the issue of breeding off daughters of slaughtered victims of the disease. British farming is staring at the prospect of slaughtering the whole herd. Only a compliant Ministry of Agriculture, a Ministry of Food trapped within its control, and a government controlled by land-owners, keep the lid on an explosive issue – can humans catch mad cow disease from milk or beef? **[184]** Gallup (1990). Nearly one-tenth of the national population. The current Secretary of State for Agriculture, Fisheries and Food appointed himself 'green' minister in his own department, under the government's programme of appointing environmentally-briefed ministers in each department of state. He has actively promoted the spread of hamburger fast foods and the eating of beef possibly tainted with mad cow disease. **[185]** *The Grocer.* **[186]** *The Grocer.* **[187]** RM/British Plastics Federation. Over a stone, about the weight of two domestic vacuum cleaners. **[188]** British Plastics Federation (1990). Food and drink now takes more than a third of the 1.3m tons of plastic used in British packaging. Plastic replaces cans, glass and paper, and whether it is more environmentally desirable is a highly complex question that goes to the heart of Product Life Cycle Analysis and 'green' labelling. The whole cradle-to-grave production and distribution picture has to be taken into account, raising profound questions about our industrial system, waste disposal and methods of accounting and government. **[189]** *The Grocer*. Marfona potatoes sell for 33 pence each at Marks & Spencer 'speciality' food stores. They are sold in a clamshell-shaped PVC tray (unmarked with polymer category), wrapped in PVC cling film, with a liveried label marked 'Marfona baking potatoes smooth creamy texture'. **[190]** Euromonitor/RM. By selling tea in bags and by brand names, importers conceal from consumers the true origins of teas, with a resultant widespread ignorance about the effects of our tannin- and caffeine-habit on poor countries whose economies are grossly distorted by tea crops. See R. North, *The Real Cost*. Juggernauts of tea consumed in the UK in a year would stretch 78 miles nose-to-tail. **[191]** MAFF/RM. Britain has a huge 'ghost' acreage abroad supporting its massive over-population of energy-guzzling consumers. Workers on Britain's hidden plantations often work under semi-slavery conditions even worse than those on the farms of the National Farmers Union. **[192]** *New Book of World Rankings*. Sean Ryan, in *The Sunday Times*, writes that '45 per cent of the ancient woods (in Britain) has been cut down in the past 50 years' (31 May 1992). **[193]** *New Book of World Rankings*. South Americans respond to northern criticism of the felling of ancient forests by saying: 'what about you?' Trees are still felled more frequently in the USA than in Brazil. **[194]** *New Book of World Rankings*. Boar and bear were hunted all over the country 25 generations ago. What does that suggest for 25 generations hence? **[195]** Ramblers Association/RM. **[196]** Ramblers Association. One woodland acre in 243 is accessible. **[197]** Ramblers Association. A total of 382,000 acres. **[198]** RM/Dept of Transport, 1989. Total ton-kilometres was 176.7bn. **[199]** RM/Dept of Transport, 1989. Total ton-kilometres was 219.9bn. Population increase is allowed, from 55m to 56.5m. Rail freight declined from 363m ton-km per capita to 318m over the same decade. **[200]** RM/Dept of Transport, 1989. 126bn ton-kilometres, down from 130bn in 1990, a clear case of recession sparing the environment. **[201]** Dept of transport, 1989. 99bn ton-kilometres. This is not all carried by juggernauts, which are used only as a handy visualiser. **[202]** Road Freight Association (to 1990). **[203]** Freight Transport Association. **[204]** Dept of Energy. **[205]** Dept of Energy. A power utility in Canada pays customers to turn in old appliances. A similar scheme is in place in Wisconsin, USA. It is, of course, cheaper to reduce consumption than to build new power stations (leaving out the environment). **[206]** Lang & Clutterbuck, *P Is For Pesticides* (1989). In 1988/9 Ministry of Agriculture tests, 38 per cent of samples contained residues. **[207]** Dept of Energy (1991). **[208]** Dept of Energy (1991). So much for energy conservation! **[209]** *The Grocer*. But only 20 per cent of a given bottle is recycled cullet. Locally-filled bring-back containers are the ecological way forward. **[210]** *The Grocer.* **[211]** British Plastics Federation. 1990 market estimated at 46,150,000 tons, used chiefly in contact moulding processes. **[212]** RM/Countryside Commission. **[213]** James Wilkinson. **[214]** RM/MAFF (1980–89). Methane is a powerful greenhouse-effect gas. **[215]** RM/Dept of the Environment. Emissions would fill a 13-mile queue of nose-to-tail road tankers each day, and a year's pollution would stretch 4,839 miles, or one-fifth of the way round the world. **[216]** Lord President. **[217]** Hansard. An effort to update this 1991 information from the Lord President resulted in two stalled calls via 071-219 3000 to the Parliamentary information service, a refusal to discuss the question from the Sergeant-At-Arms office, and no answer on another switchboard given as the Lord President's office. Who was it that suggested the Palace of Westminster should become a theme park and the government moved to Canary Wharf? **[218]** Cabinet Office (1991). The government stationery office spent £93,000 just publishing the shorter version of the Charter. **[219]** Civil Service. 36,004 were scrapped, or 4,500 for every year involved. **[220]** HMSO (1986–91). **[221]** Civil Service. Supposedly post-automation, there is a Revenue staff member for every 953 Britons, man, woman and child. There is one for every 385 members of the working population. Self-reporting, which has been the practice in North America for decades, is still not permitted to the British, who are patronised like untrustworthy children. The self-employed sector, which increased by about 1m during the 1980s, is particularly badly catered for by this service which, above all, is run by Parliament. **[222]** Dept of Social Security. **[223]**Dept of Education. **[224]** Dept of Education. **[225]** Welsh Office (1990). **[226]** Northern Ireland Office. **[227]** BBC Radio 5, News (1992). **[228]** MORI. This 1990 survey finding may seem out of tune with subsequent economic setbacks, but during the crash of 1991 MORI was still finding in a comprehensive survey that pollution ranked fourth, above education, among people's chief concerns. Defence and foreign affairs came bottom, with a statistically negligible 2 per cent (MORI, *Typically British?* 1991). **[229]** CND. **[230]** Mental Health Association (1989 estimate). **[231]** Dept of Health/ RM. **[232]** OPCS. **[233]** Dept of Health/RM (1990). About 575m tablets per year (at 25 per prescription), or 11 per British adult. **[234]** Ramblers Association. **[235]** Dept of the Environment. *English House Condition Survey* (1986). A Spring 1992 City survey estimated 1.8m households to be paying off mortgages greater than the current sellable value of their house. **[236]** British Plastics Federation. Expanded polystyrene is used to make hamburger boxes, huge numbers of which are expected to be littered across Eastern Europe and Asia in the next few years. Gross tonnage is deceptive, as EPS is very light. Its massive use in housing may have undiscovered health contraindications. About 64 per cent goes into housing, 32 per cent into packaging, much of the latter ending up in landfills or as litter. A new application for EPS is infill material in road-building. Exports growing. **[237]** Dept of the Environment. **[238]** Dept of the Environment. **[239]**Dept of Social Security. This amount would have built 1,640 £35,000 flats. **[240]** DSS. **[241]** Treasury. **[242]** Home Office. Following integration of EC states' borders. **[243]** RM/Dept of the Environment, *Digest of Environmental Water Statistics*, 1989. This volume may be inflated by its inclusion of water used for cooling. The heating of the water, though, remains a form of pollution. **[244]** *British Airways Fact Book*, 1991. 271,000 flights 1990–91. Route-passenger-kms grew in 1990 by 16.6 per cent worldwide. At that growth rate, world air travel would double in under five years. Environment is literally the last word in BA's 75-word statement of missions and goals. No other mention is made of the topic in the company's 1991 Fact Book. One of BA's 50 jumbo jets burns 160 tons of aviation fuel in a 16-hour flight, or more than five road tanker loads, five miles high, spewing into Earth's immune system hydrocarbons with unknown effects. **[245]** Home Office. This must be one of the most revealing figures of the Margaret Thatcher prime ministership. The so-called 'Chinese wall' supposed to exist between the banking and brokering arms of post-Big Bang financial services companies is obviously a massive confidence trick. Company boards would be answerable to their stockholders if they failed to profit from insider knowledge. The conflict of interest is glaring, which is why Britain did not allow it for two hundred years. Dyfed prosecutes more fraud than the City police. **[246]** Home Office. Fifteen per cent of prisoners, though, are still forced into a grotesque scrum to be first in the morning to slop out their bucket of excrement. That's 6,750 men, or five times the population of Eton. **[247]** Home Office. **[248]** Ministry of Defence. **[249]** M. Chisholm and P. Kivell, *Inner City Waste Land* (1987). A total of 11,630 hectares. Hyde Park is 341 acres. **[250]** Dept of the Environment, *Review of Derelict Land Policy* (1988). Hyde Park is 341 acres. Total derelict is 40,489 hectares. **[251]** Nature Conservancy Council. Peat is bagged and sold in garden centres for fertiliser. Incredibly, much of it is actually transported from Finland. Obviously, gardens should be fertilised with household compost, not landscape torn up thousands of miles away, or even in Ireland. Fisons, the chemicals corporation, in 1992 sold its composting business because of the bad publicity. **[252]** Land Registry. An area of 82,400 acres: enough for 494,000 one-sixth acre plots. **[253]** Inland Revenue. **[254]** Dept of the Environment, *Review of Derelict Land Policy* (1988). **[255]** David Cannadine. **[256]** OPCS. **[257]** Scottish Office. **[258]** Dept of Health (1991 in England and Wales). A total of 202,626 English and Welsh mental handicap and illness cases were discharged from hospitals in 1988–9, supposedly 'into the community', although the hospitals themselves had been built by 'the community' to deal with the patients' suffering, and they could have been considered to have been 'in the community' while in hospital and strictly speaking 'out of the community' when evicted. **[259]** Dept of Transport. **[260]**

Euromonitor. **[261]** Road Freight Association. **[262]** Earth Resources Research (1991). Current traffic managers think in terms of cutting travel time. They seem unable to consider the other side of the equation, which is creating distance. **[263]** Freight Transport Association (1988). Down from 7,800 in 1975. **[264]** Silk, *How Parliament Works* (1990). **[265]** Silk, *How Parliament Works* (1990). **[266]** Law Society's *Gazette* (to 31 Sept 91). **[267]** Law Society's *Gazette* (to 31 Sept 91). **[268]** Ministry of Arts and Libraries. **[269]** Ministry of Arts and Libraries. **[270]** Scottish Office. Peter Duesberg, a US authority on viruses, argues that drug abuse causes some of the deaths identified as Aids, not HIV. **[271]** Dept of Health. **[272]** Welsh Office (1992). A total of 186,519 acres. **[273]** RM/ Dept of Energy. A complex formula known as the Nuclear Levy, whereby the government subsidises uninsurable and uneconomic nuclear-power stations through a levy on thermal-power generation. It is not quite as simple as a 10 per cent levy on each bill, because 18.4 per cent (*The Economist*) of electricity is nuclear-powered, but that's the jist of it. Green auditing often makes economic nonsense of conventional cost- ings: nuclear power is already recognised as unviable – if you leave out the weapons factor. **[274]** Pierre Tangay. **[275]** RM/Dept of Energy. **[276]** *Time*/RM. **[277]** Dept of Energy (1990). Allow some extra tons to update the figure. Spent fuel is refined into plutonium, the key ingredient in hydrogen bombs. Negotiations are under way to import spent fuel from South Korea, a state involved in a nuclear weapons race with communist North Korea. The juggernauts of spent fuel imported into Britain so far would stretch nearly two miles nose-to-tail, taking about 45 minutes to walk past. **[278]** RM/estimated from official figures (1985/6). An Olympic- sized swimming-poolful every two years. **[279]** Dept of Energy. **[280]** Dept of Energy (1990). **[281]** Ministry of Transport (1990). **[282]** Dept of Transport. Every weekday totals 103. **[283]** Dept of Health (1990). **[284]** *The Grocer*. **[285]** Dept of Health (1990–91). The equivalent of two-thirds of the population visit public hospital out-patient departments each year. **[286]** Dept of Health (1992). Upper atmosphere chlorine levels were reported to be 70 times natural levels during the winter of 1991–2, increasing ultra-violet light from the sun, which causes eye cataracts and skin cancer. **[287]** Dept of Health. **[288]** *The Grocer*. About level with the gross domestic product of prosperous Uraguay. Down with the recession to £3,769m in 1990/91. **[289]** Euromonitor (1990). **[290]** Euromonitor (1990). **[291]** Lord President of the Council (1991). Seven juggernaut loads. **[292]** Dept of the Environment (1.46m tons 1988). **[293]** *Materials Reclamation Weekly*. **[294]** *Materials Reclamation Weekly*. **[295]** Euro- monitor/RM. A year's flushing would fill nose-to-tail juggernauts for 138 miles. **[296]** Science in Parliament. So much for Mrs Thatcher's miracle. **[297]** Science in Parliament. **[298]** National Poisons Unit, evidence to House of Commons Agriculture Committee, 1987. **[299]** Lang and Clut- terbuck, *P Is For Pesticides* (1991). A small farm's pesticide use may not be inspected more than once every 28 years, the authors report. 142 inspectors cover 300,000 premises and 700,000 workers. Between January '89 and March '90, 29 cases were brought under Control of Pesticides Regulations. **[300]** Lang and Clutterbuck, *P Is For Pesticides* (1991). Nearly one kilo per acre per year on Britain's 42m farmed acres. **[301]** MAFF. John Button, in *Green Magazine*, cites the British Field Sports Association's *Hunting: The Facts* saying roughly 18,000 foxes are killed by hunts with hound packs each year. Another 150,000 are killed each year by humans. No wonder the suburbs are full of them: they're refugees! **[302]** *Media Register*. **[303]** *Media Register*. By 1991 these budgets were down to £15,000,000 (£8,560,000 for petrol, £6,635,000 for oil), and Saatchi & Saatchi were losing £212,000 a day, which nevertheless did not prevent the bosses paying themselves £1,200 a day basic each. Nor, of course, did it prevent the inexorable depletion of a fossil resource that took 250,000 years to form. **[304]** *Book of World Rankings*. **[305]** *Book of World Rankings*. **[306]** CSO. **[307]** CSO. **[308]** Dept of Health. **[309]** Dept of Health. **[310]** British Plastics Federation (1990). Up 48 per cent since 1986. **[311]** British Plastics Federation (1990). A total of 30,750 tons. Cling film has been officially declared 'prudent to avoid' for health as a wrapping for fatty foods, but avoidance appears negligible to shoppers. After wrapping cheese, sausages and dozens of other foods, most of it goes to landfill sites, where it takes many years to decompose, releasing its suspect 'plasticiser' chemicals. **[312]** Plants outnumber plastics recycling plants by about 3,960. **[313]** British Plastics Federation. Film and sheeting forms 75 per cent of low/linear low-density polyethylene production, which totals 540,000 tons a year (1990). Growth has been slowed by environmental pressures, causing substitution by other polymers, notably polypropylene. **[314]** British Plastics Federation. Sheer ugliness has slowed growth in plastic window-frame and door sales, as their incompatibility with older building styles has been gradually recognised. Windows and doors form 18 per cent of the 615,000-ton annual PVC consumption. PVC production involves huge amounts of environmentally undesirable chlorine, with extremely toxic and carcinogenic by-products that it also releases on incineration. **[315]** IstoE-Señhor 29/389, cited in S. Nugent, *Big Mouth: The Amazon Speaks*. **[316]** *Materials Reclamation Weekly*. Wellman International Ltd, bottle recyclers of Kells, Co. Meath, put the number at 20,000. Definition of a bottle is part of the problem. Wellman can process 12,000 tons of scrap bottles. Unfortunately, Irish environmentalists complain that Wellman collects few Irish bottles! **[317]** *Materials Reclamation Weekly*. **[318]** RM/British Plastics Federation (1991). Plastics form 35.7 per cent of UK packaging. The industry says without plastics, the packaging industry would consume twice as much energy, packaging waste would increase 150 per cent by volume and 300 per cent by weight. However, not a word in the industry's latest *Statistics Handbook* (1990–91) is devoted to recycling, and the Life Cycle Analysis of plastics remains bad. Annual weight of plastic packaging produced is 1.3m tons. **[319]** Cartridge Care, St Helens/RM. This responsible firm is trying to recycle its disposables. **[320]** J. Sainsbury. **[321]** RECOUP. 35 pilot schemes are in operation, but the future of plastics recycling is marred by the large variety of polymers in use. **[322]** Home Office (sample figure from 1991). **[323]** Green Line. About £150m worth (Euromonitor 1992 pro-rated from 1989 at 5 per cent) of bleach and toilet cleaners are sold per year, or 87,000 tons. **[324]** MORI. **[325]** *The Grocer*. **[326]** RM/Dept of Transport. Sulphur dioxide causes acid rain, which is exported to Scandinavia, where 3,000 lakes have had to be treated with lime in an effort to restore life. 14,000 lakes are said to be dead. **[327]** RM/Dept of Transport. More than 25,000 road-tanker loads a year, which would stretch 240 miles nose-to-tail. Many of them rise slowly to the upper atmosphere and interfere with the planet's immune system. Car drivers kill planets. **[328]** RM/D. Taufel, *The Social Costs of Road Transport of Goods* (1989). **[329]** RM/D. Taufel, *The Social Costs of Road Transport of Goods* (1989). The figures apply strictly to West Germany but correspond broadly to the rest of northern Europe. 'The proportion of goods carried by rail rather than road is nearly three times higher in France and Germany than in Britain,' *Reviving The City*, Friends of the Earth, (1991). **[330]** Dept of Transport/RM. A total of 525 road tanker loads, or 1,815 miles of them nose-to-tail per year. Carbon monoxide is a deadly poison, colourless and odourless. **[331]** Dept of Transport. **[332]** Dept of the Environment. **[333]** Dept of the Environment. **[334]** Green Party. **[335]** Green Party. **[336]** Census/RM. **[337]** Census/RM. **[338]** DSS. **[339]** DSS. Here is the budget for restoring people to the land. **[340]** DSS. **[341]** DSS. **[342]** Dept of Transport (1989). **[343]** Dept of Transport (1989). **[344]** Dept of Transport (1990). **[345]** Dept of Transport (1990). **[346]** Dept of Transport. **[347]** Scottish Office. **[348]** Dept of Transport. **[349]** S. Counsell, *Good Wood Guide* (1989). Counsell considers that only 0.2 per cent of all tropical moist forests are being managed sustainably. Great Britain is Europe's largest importer of tropical hardwoods. Fifty per cent of it is estimated to be used by the construction industry. **[350]** WANA: Cynghair Wrth Niwclear Cymreig. In 1990 the assets of operator Nuclear Electric were £6,300m, and liabilities, including fuel reprocessing, storage and decommissioning: £9,551m. **[351]** *The Grocer*. **[352]** *The Grocer*. About 22m energy-intensive aluminium cans are thrown away every day. **[353]** RM/Dept of the Environment (1990). **[354]** RM/BT *Business Pages*, London, 1992 (pop. 6.4m). There are 150,000 population served by each of the public waste recycling depots licensed by the London Waste Regulation Authority. Charity shops such as Oxfam serve as recycling businesses for clothing and household items. **[355]** *The Grocer*. A total of 9,200m steel cans are used per year in drinks, pet food and human food. Ten per cent get recycled. The target for 2000 is 50 per

SOURCES & NOTES [356]–[390]

cent, but much stricter EC targets can be expected by 1993/4. Every day 22m are thrown away. **[356]** SCPR. **[357]** SCPR. **[358]** Eurostat. Gross research-and-development funds in France are ECU11.1bn per year. It has to be remembered that intra-Euro state statistical comparisons may be unreliable because of methodological differences, but when the gulf is as great as that between France and Britain the matter is certainly worth attention. The disparity reflects the huge cost of France's continuing quest for superstate status – its (suspended) Pacific nuclear bomb testing, its armageddon submarines, and so on – compared with Britain's partial status as a US client. **[359]** Eurostat. Gross figure for Britain is ECU7.3bn per annum. **[360]** RM/*Reviving The City*, Friends of the Earth, from Dept of the Environment figures (1985). **[361]** Dept of Transport. **[362]** Dept of Transport. **[363]** Dept of Transport. Daily spending on new roads per ton of carbon monoxide emitted by vehicles is £323. The secretary of state for transport said in 1992 that road-building was environmentally friendly. Wouldn't it be nice to have a government? **[364]** BBC Radio 4, *File on Four*. There were 5,000 of these nominee money-laundering and tax-avoiding instruments in 1986, according to the BBC. **[365]** RM/A *Guide to Company Giving* (1991). **[366]** RM/Treasury. **[367]** Treasury. **[368]** HM Treasury (1992 pro rata 1989). **[369]** Treasury/RM (1990). **[370]** Household survey. **[371]** Eurostat. **[372]** Eurostat. In spite of Britons' waste flow being so much lighter than Americans', due to restricted space the UK faces an equally serious waste volume crisis. **[373]** Dept of Education. **[374]** Dept of Education and Science. **[375]** Dept of Education and Science (1991). **[376]** Dept of Education. **[377]** Dept of Education and Science. **[378]** Dept of Education. **[379]** Dept of Education and Science (1991). **[380]** *The Bookseller* (1991). **[381]** Dept of Education and Science. **[382]** Dept of Energy. **[383]** Dept of Energy. **[384]** House of Commons Environment Committee (1989). The EC may soon stop the sea-dumping (30 per cent) of sludge, contaminated by heavy metals and other hazardous agents. Doubts are also expressed about spreading most of the rest of it agriculturally, up to 9.8m tons out of an annual total of some 14m tons, although the composting principle is good. **[385]** *Population Trends* (1989). Every day, over 300 parents on average mess up their children's lives. In-depth, long-term research by child-rearing expert Penelope Leach has revealed the toxic shame caused in children by divorce, the damaging of their performance, and their loss of advantages later in life. **[386]** David Alton, MP/RM. Many foetuses find their way into hospital waste and are incinerated. **[387]** MORI, *Typically British?* (1991). **[388]** *Population Trends* (1989). Over 700 per working day. **[389]** Campaign Against Pornography and Censor-ship. The reported daily income of *Sunday Sport* smut-rag publisher David Sullivan was in 1989/90 reported to be £7,923 (see entry 504). The slump in ad. sales may have reduced the amount. **[390]** *The Whole Thing*. About £251m (1992 pro rata 1990 [Euromonitor]) a year is spent on female sanitary wear, virtually all of which is 'disposable'. The pinkish removable adhesive strip cover featured on the pantyliner-type pad adorns the beaches and riverbanks of Britain in its millions. At 13 pads per capita, annual disposal in an urbanised globe of 6bn would be 78bn. **[391]** Dept of Health. **[392]** Dept of Health. **[393]** Dept of Health. **[394]** Dept of Health. **[395]** MORI (1991). **[396]** MORI. **[397]** MORI. **[398]** Dept of Energy. Britain may not seem the most obvious place to research solar power, but even a cloudy day gives light. End-user solar power has an important role to play in reducing mains-power consumption. Spending on solar power is one-forty-seventh of what is spent on nuclear power. **[399]** Dept of Energy. **[400]** R. Mabey, *Food For Free*. A microspecies has small variations within the species. Genetic engineering eliminates such microspecies, which confer hardiness. In biodiversity lies nature's greatest strength and profit's greatest enemy. **[401]** Dept of Transport (1989: 96,000,000). To Cape Town three-and-a-half times. **[402]** Dept of Transport (510,000,000 tons). Eight and a half times round the world. **[403]** Dept of Transport. (1988–9: 2,700,000 tonnes.) **[404]** MAFF. **[405]** *The Grocer*. **[406]** OPCS (1989). **[407]** OPCS (1989). **[408]** *The Stage* and *TV Today*. **[409]** RM/*The Stage* and *TV Today*. **[410]** Friends of the Earth. **[411]** Friends of the Earth. **[412]** Euromonitor. **[413]** *Social Trends*. **[414]** DTI. Ten times as much to research a war plane as to prepare to meet the future. **[415]** Dept of Energy. This is a derisory amount. Canada, already a massive hydro-electric producer, has invested in a huge tidal-power project at the Bay of Fundy and identified six other major potential sites. Salter's Duck, a major British discovery which uses dynamos that float on the sea, obviating the need for dams that silt up and interfere with marine life, was deliberately suppressed in the late 1970s by the Scottish nuclear industry. **[416]** DTI (1991). An apt exercise, perhaps, for a country with one of the highest proportions of prison inmates and convicted men anywhere outside the USA. **[417]** MAFF. **[418]** Dept of the Environment. A total of 36,789 tons in 1989/90. It is arguable that small countries not generating enough hazardous waste to be able to burn it economically are fair customers for UK incinerators, which were built earlier in the UK than in other countries – but surveys show the public does not agree. **[419]** Dept of the Environment. **[420]** Dept of the Environment. **[421]** RM/Dept of the Environment (1989–90). Most hazardous waste is dumped in landfill sites by being poured on to domestic waste, a crude technique with unknown long-term risks. Layering is being adopted at some sites, but the BMA warns that layering materials may not last more than about 30 years. **[422]** RM/CSO. US research links polycyclic aromatic hydrocarbons and lung cancer. Benzene is especially carcinogenic. Prompts drowsiness, sore eyes and coughing. The US EPA considers four in a hundred occupationally exposed to it to risk death. It seems doubly strange for imports and exports of such a dangerous substance to be duplicated (1989). **[423]** CSO (1989). **[424]**

RM/Dept of the Environment. **[425]** RM/Dept of the Environment. Most of it went to sites which an Atomic Energy Authority study (Croft and Campbell, 1990) found to be poorly monitored for environmental effects such as the contamination of ground water and build-up of landfill gas. Most sites studied were within 500 metres of residential areas. **[426]** Advertising Association (1992 extrapolated from 1990). Public interest advertising has less than one-third the budget of the motor industry alone. **[427]** *Municipal Journal*. **[428]** Home Office (sample figure from 1991). **[429]** Dept of Transport. An increase of 5,910,607, or 10,300 a week, nearly 1,500 a day. **[430]** Dept of Transport. **[431]** Dept of Transport. From reduction in wear and tear, police, rescue, etc. **[432]** Transport Statistics GB/RM. From 1963, 2,123 railway stations were closed. It is hardly surprising that lorry-blight has spread rampantly as a result. **[433]** *The Independent on Sunday* (1990). In 1980 the speed was 12.3 mph. Countless commuters are alone in their vehicles. Much new congestion has been caused by light vans, up from 155,000 in 1985 to 204,000 in 1989, an increase of over 1,000 per month. **[434]** Dept of Transport. **[435]** Dept of Transport (1989). From 378bn per year (1978) to 523bn per year (1988). Use of public service vehicles naturally declined, from 50bn passenger/km per year (1978) to 41bn (1988). **[436]** Transport Statistics GB/RM. **[437]** Dept of Transport. An increase of 50,000 hours a year, nearly 1,000 hours a week. The effect of burning Olympic-sized swimming-poolfuls of kerosene in the upper atmosphere is unknown. Europe's ultra-violet protective ozone layer was found to be depleted by 20 per cent 1991/2. Observers have sat at Alpine ski resorts and watched condensation trails criss-cross the sky until sunlight was significantly reduced by a veil of haze later in the day. Ron Muddle, chief planner at British Airways, has said he wants to make his fleet 'ozone friendly'. **[438]** Dept of Transport. **[439]** Dept of Transport. **[440]** Dept of Transport. **[441]** Dept of Transport. **[442]** Dept of Transport. An increase of 31,382 in four years, or 21 per day. **[443]** RM/*Life* magazine. **[444]** Euromonitor/RM (1989). **[445]** Euromonitor/RM. Some £850,000 of it per day is for cars, petrol or oil. **[446]** CPC. **[447]** RM/CSO. **[448]** *The Timetables of History*. Population is officially censussed in 1988 at 57m, now possibly closer to 59m (if growing at 1 per cent), a 10m to 59m population boom which official forecasts predict levelling out, possibly contracting very slightly, but remaining above 50m for the foreseeable future. Government policy seems incapable of evaluating the desirable carrying capacity of the land and strategies aimed at achieving the resultant population goal. **[449]** *Social Trends*. **[450]** RM/CSO. **[451]** National Audit Office. This represents only a fraction of the plane, mainly the wings. **[452]** Ministry of Defence (1991). **[453]** Exchequer. **[454]** Ministry of Defence (1992 extrapolated from 1991). It seems extravagant for nearly £2m a day of taxes to be spent with no open accountability. **[455]** Ministry of Defence (1989–90). **[456]** Ministry of Defence (1990). Britain's high-tech workforce has been described as 'trapped' in the military-industrial complex, upon which 500,000 jobs depend. **[457]** Dept of Defence (1991). Some 10,000 pubs were reported empty by Shelter, the housing campaign group, in 1992. **[458]** Ministry of Defence. Extrapolated from 3,596 complaints in first six months of 1991. Tornado low-flying attack methods were proven a notable failure in the 1991 bombing attacks on Iraq, with a high loss of the almost incalculably expensive multinational aircraft. Low-flying practices are being slightly modified by the RAF. **[459]** RM/CSO. **[460]** CND *Today*. **[461]** CND. Each Trident originally had 128 warheads, but the total is subject to current adjustment. **[462]** British Army of the Rhine/RM. (1992 pro-rated from 1990). Firing one is even more expensive: a shell costs £550 (BAOR). **[463]** Ministry of Defence. **[464]** *Information Please Almanac 1992* (1990). **[465]** UK Central Information Office (1990). The US defence budget is 87 per cent of the UK's national budget. **[466]** Ministry of Defence. **[467]** Ministry of Defence. **[468]** *House of Commons Environment Committee Second Report, Session 1988/9* Toxic Waste (estimate). Cited in the BMA's *Hazardous Waste and Human Health*, the estimate includes toxics, hazardous, and household, agricultural and building wastes, and sewage sludge. **[469]** British Medical Association/London Waste Regulation Authority (1987–8). A total of 30,000 tons, or 1,364 juggernaut loads. Ninety per cent came from NHS hospitals and clinics. The BMA reports that bigger hospitals have been shown to produce more waste per bed than smaller ones. Only 1–2 per cent of hazardous wastes are incinerated in Britain today. Most goes to landfill sites. **[470]** Dept of the Environment. A 73-mile queue of nose-to-tail juggernaut loads, including tens of thousands of aborted foetuses. Incinerators may give off deadly dioxins and furans. **[471]** Dept of the Environment. **[472]** Geographical/RM. They would stretch 10 miles nose-to-tail. **[473]** Patrick Moore and Eugene Hargrove, *Beyond Spaceship Earth*. Moore, in his TV programme *The Sky At Night*, put the figure at 20,000. Hargrove puts pieces of junk 'larger than 1cm' in orbit at the higher figure. There is also a 'junk haze' of microscopic metallic particles caused by rocket bursts and explosions. The US Pentagon has detonated three nuclear explosions in space. **[474]** British Plastics Federation (1990). Thirty-seven per cent of injection moulding (64 per cent of total) and 64 per cent of extrusion (64 per cent of total) out of an annual total of 205,000 tons, an increase of 8 per cent over the previous year. Some bottom-of-the-range applications now employ recycled polystyrene, but most of the 4,504 annual juggernaut loads ends up in landfill, where it takes about 500 years to decompose. Polystyrene can be seen on most beaches, in rivers and floating far out to sea. **[475]** British Plastics Federation. Very little of the recyclable PET used to make plastic bottles is actually recycled, because rubbish separation is negligible and plastic recycling programmes few. The one in Milton Keynes is a pioneer. PET is gradually replacing hard-to-recycle plastics in such products as electrical plugs, sockets, connectors and printed circuit boards. **[476]** Dept of the Environment (1992/3). **[477]** Dept of the Environment (1992/3). **[478]** *The Grocer*. (1992 pro rated from 1990 at five per cent). **[479]** Scottish Office. **[480]** Euromonitor/RM. Thirteen road tankers of it (32 miles of them nose-to-tail each year) poured into drains. Most washing up can be adequately performed with plain cold water – but who will pay for messages to that effect on television? **[481]** Dept of the Environment (1990). Unsurprisingly, reports were coming out in 1992 of massive profit gouging and boss payoffs by the water monopolies. **[482]** *The Grocer*. **[483]** *The Grocer*. **[484]** DTI. **[485]** BBC *Today*. **[486]** Public Bodies (1989). **[487]** Public Bodies (1989). **[488]** Dept of Health. **[489]** Home Office. **[490]** Home Office. **[491]** DSS. **[492]** DSS. **[493]** Dept of Education. **[494]** Dept of Education. **[495]** Foreign and Commonwealth Office/RM. **[496]** Foreign and Commonwealth Office (1991). **[497]** Dept of Employment. **[498]** Dept of Employment. **[499]** Dept of Employment (1989). **[500]** Dept of Employment (1989). **[501]** Graef S. Crystal (based on $2.8m p.a.). This includes benefits. **[502]** *British Medical Journal* (based on £29,273 p.a. 60-hour week full shift). **[503]** Dept of Employment. **[504]** *GQ*/RM. **[505]** Ministry of Defence. **[506]** Agricultural Wages Board. **[507]** Exchequer (1990–91). **[508]** *GQ*/RM. The reported annual salary of 41-year-old David Verey, chairman of Lazard Brothers, is £1,120,000. **[509]** *New Statesman & Society*. **[510]** *New Statesman & Society*. **[511]** Exchequer. **[512]** O.M. Lewis/Home Office. **[513]** Treasury (1992–3). **[514]** BBC *Today*. Over 2m jobs were converted to peaceful purposes 1945–50. There is no reason a conversion one quarter of the scale should present any difficulty in the 1990s, following the end of the Cold War. Big growth is needed in such industries as lightweight materials, solar energy, intensive farming, phytotronics, systems analysis, and so on. Only the political will is required. Why do governments always lag 30 years behind the people? **[515]** G. Leach, *Energy and Food Production* (1975). **[516]** G. Leach, *Energy and Food Production* (1975). **[517]** *Warmer Bulletin*. Sixty per cent of UK fizzy soft drinks were sold in returnable containers in 1977 – only 19 per cent 12 years later in 1987. The drinks industry simply uses local-authority rubbish lorries as free taxis to dispose of their profit-making packaging for them – which is to say, Council Tax payers directly subsidise the profits of Coca Cola, etc. A zugzwang is a chess move you're forced to make even though it's a bad one – like throwing away plastic bottles!

EURO ZONE **[518]** UN Economic Commission for Europe (1989), cited in *Worldwatch Paper 99*. **[519]** Dr Volker Beer, cited in *Worldwatch Paper 99*. **[520]** *The Lancet*. **[521]** *The Lancet*. **[522]** Predicast/Aushandel (1991). **[523]** Predicast/Aushandel (1991). These figures (in constant dollars) show a grisly doubling of expenditure that graphically displays the current proliferation of the aged and the prolongation of their senility.

The 'disposability' of the pads is, of course, likely to be fallacious. There are about 61,000 centenarians in the USA. Helena Norberg Hodge, in her book *Ancient Futures*, describes the people of Ladakh as living vigorous, songful lives and working all their days until they drop. A long, semi-crippled geriatric phase is unknown. **[524]** Martin Parry. The EC already has a large budget devoted to combatting the spread of the Sahara desert into southern Europe. **[525]** *Farmers Weekly*. US studies have shown organic and chemical or low-chemical farming to be equally productive. **[526]** RM/MAFF (1990). This is a sample of the many strange subsidies in the complicated Common Agricultural Plan of the EC, whereby farmers literally plough their own feather-bed. The Spanish eat about 91 kg of rice per capita, the British 3.8 kg. **[527]** Euromonitor, *European Marketing Data and Statistics* (1992). Anyone can see that each ton of rice has a £32.75 subsidy on it, or 3p per kilo. Why 3p? Why not 0p? Alternatively, why not free rice? Welcome to the CAP! **[528]** Ministry of Overseas Development. **[529]** RM/EC Commission. **[530]** Gosplan report, cited in *Worldwatch Paper 99*. **[531]** RM/Economist Intelligence Unit. This is symptomatic of the USA's fossil-fuel decadence. Much cargo went in proliferating passenger holds. Figures were 5,737bn ton-km (1984), rising to 7,912bn ton-km (1989). But growth elsewhere is demented, too. Although the effect of exhaust gases on the atmosphere is little understood, IATA predicts 6 per cent per year world growth, or a doubling in 11.6 years. Growth in North East Asia is put at 9.7 per cent, or doubling in 7 years. British Airways' privatisation shareholders have shrunk from 1.1m at launch to 296,000 in 1991. **[532]** RM/Statistical Abstract of the US/Survey of Current Business. A near-doubling of international air cargo in five years. One of the most revealing fossil fuel-addiction figures of our age. Possibly a phenomenon that will never be matched, at least until totally new forms of propulsion are discovered. *British Airways News* (20 March 1992) states: 'The effect of exhaust gases on the atmosphere is not well understood.' British Airways tops the world revenue-ton-km freight league, with double United Airlines' figure. **[533]** Dept of the Environment (22 Oct 1990). Germany and the Netherlands' per capita recycling of aluminium is reckoned to be twice as good as Great Britain's. **[534]** OECD. A total of 50,000m aluminium cans are thrown away world-wide each year, or 137m a day – and that's with 50 per cent recycling! Euro recycling is only 40 per cent (ACRA), which means that of the 18,000m produced per year, nearly 11,000m are thrown away. 35,000m are expected to be used per year in 2000, which means that at a higher recycling rate, say 60 per cent, 14,000m would still be thrown away every year, or 38m per day. Is this really acceptable? Should consumers not insist on bringing back the 'bring-back' container? **[535]** Dept of the Environment (22 Oct 1990). **[536]** *Worldwatch Paper 99*. Hungary has also lost 40 plant species. **[537]** RM/Statistical Abstract of the US. Each American's average share of US energy consumed in

1990 was 328,000,000 BTU, equivalent to about 328,000 cu ft of gas, (which actually formed about 24 per cent of all consumption). Per capita energy consumption has slightly decreased (by 0.6 per cent) since 1970 – but the consuming population has increased by 53m or 25 per cent. Expressed in SI, each American consumes 346,040m joules (Canadians more), the highest consumption of any industrialised country. **[538]** Euromonitor (1990). The UK is above the EC average with 13.4, the US stands at 15.9. Consuming 100 times as much energy as Asians, Europeans can be considered to have a Third World equivalent population of about 3bn. **[539]** Euromonitor (1990). **[540]** *Worldwatch Paper 99*. Most is delivered by the Danube and Dnieper Rivers. Another 4,300 tonnes of nitrogen compounds, 900 tonnes of petroleum products and 200 tonnes of detergents from industrial wastes are reckoned to enter the Black Sea each year. **[541]** Euromonitor. The highest car penetration in the world. And yet, Rome has cleared its centre of private traffic. No British city has. **[542]** *Reviving the City*, Friends of the Earth (1991). Two million cars enter Greater Paris every day. Tailbacks of headlights are to be seen at 6am on commuter motorways. French petrol is about eight per cent more expensive than Britain's, and France has no oil wells. **[543]** DRI (1992 estimate). A total 405m tonnes of water are polluted washing their components. Also, great quantities of solvents, vaporous paints, electricity, etc., are used – all before pollutant fuel meets motor. **[544]** *Worldwatch Paper 99*. **[545]** Eurostat. **[546]** *Quid* encyclopaedia (Paris, 1989). **[547]** Dept of the Environment. **[548]** RM/Predicast/*Fortune* (1991). 25m units in 26 per cent of US households. Another 30–40 football fields in Canada. **[549]** *British Airways Fact Book* (1991). The effects of burning 22,500 gals (82t) of jet fuel in the upper atmosphere between London and New York are unknown, but BA Concordes do it four times a day. In BA's fleet, they average 17 years old. How safe would you feel, travelling very fast in a car made in 1975? How would you feel, on a three-quarters-full plane (75), using up enough petrol in eight hours, to do 21,000 miles in your car (at 35 mpg)? Concorde uses twice the fuel per hour of a jumbo jet, for nearly a quarter the passengers. **[550]** Simon Wolff, *New Scientist* (1992). **[551]** Dept of Environment/Hansard Parliamentary Written Answers. **[552]** *Time*. **[553]** *Paris Match*. **[554]** *Campaign*. **[555]** *Campaign*. **[556]** OECD. **[557]** Economist Intelligence Unit 1990–91. Measures to combat global warming and ozone-layer loss alone will tend to switch defence and pollution-control budget proportions over the next century, as the industrial system's defence against attack is transformed into its defence against self-destruction. **[558]** *Aerospace Facts and Figures* (1990–91) page 50. An average of 4,564 per state in three years. **[559]** RM/Euromonitor's *Consumer USA*. The US National Inst. on Drug Abuse puts regular marijuana users in the USA at 9.7m. Forty-three different brands of diazepam tranquilliser are available. When Roche lost its Valium monopoly in 1985, its prescriptions stood at

15m a year, or 58,000 a working day. **[560]** RM/Euromonitor. **[561]** RM/ *Canada Yearbook* (1992). Or 48,857 km, easily girdling the globe. Forty-seven per cent of it, or 14,262 miles of 18-wheelers, goes to the USA: 70.5m tons (1989). Canada's known commercial coal reserves (6bn tons) will currently last 86 years. Another 30bn tons, not fully delineated, may never be commercially viable. Coal burning gives off dioxins (poisons), carbon dioxide (greenhouse effect) and sulphur (acid rain). Systems used are usually extremely inefficient, wasting as much as one-third of the available calories through the stack. **[562]** Predicast/Appliance Manufacturer (1991). Current sales are 67,403 a week. All contain materials dangerous to the ozone layer, and are widely serviced by bleeding them off. **[563]** Economist Intelligence Unit. On current usage at current estimated reserves. The US economy already relies on imports for half its oil. Suppose it is relying on Persian Gulf reserves for 95 per cent of its oil and there is an interruption of delivery? **[564]** RM/Economist Intelligence Unit. This must be at least halved within a generation. **[565]** *Aerospace Facts and Figures* (1991). Missile and conservation spends provide a harsh comparison with grim implications – politicians spend nearly four times as much developing attack missiles as learning how to prepare for the future. In 1988 US Presidential Candidate Albert Gore proposed a global Strategic Environmental Initiative. He may be written to at the Senate, Capitol Hill, Washington, DC, USA. **[566]** Predicast (1992). **[567]** OECD Economic Survey. The farmer usually has a severe backache problem, not from heavy lifting, but from constant driving in a sealed cab with loud music playing. **[568]** RM/Statistical Abstract of the US. The loss to the environment of such guardians is severe. Corporately-managed farms alone are proliferating rapidly. **[569]** Predicast/Env Chem/Chem Ind (1991/90). Annual growth of fertiliser is 6 per cent, and of nitrogen plant food 2.6 per cent. Would stretch from Tierra Del Fuego nearly as far as Prudhoe Bay in trucks each year – not counting Canada. **[570]** Predicast/Feedstuffs. New York City to Los Angeles and back two and a half times. The waste of resources on meat protein is tremendous. The Japanese, who show no signs of fading away, eat 7.8 kg of beef per capita, compared with an American's 47.3 and a Canadian's 39.0. The population of India also thriving, eats 0.3 kg (Euromonitor) per capita. Yet US meat production is growing at 3.1 per cent a year, with meat advertising spend up 12.4 per cent a year to combat consumers' dietary compunctions (Predicast). **[571]** RM/Euromonitor (1990). A total of 30.5m tons. **[572]** RM/Euromonitor (1990). A total of 2.1m tons. **[573]** RM/Euromonitor. Three million Mars bars are eaten per day in the UK. **[574]** RM/Predicast/PlasRubr. A total of 32.7bn a year, more than double the 1980 figure. **[575]** *The Independent.* A plant exists in Ireland, and more are planned. PET bottles are currently recycled at a percentage rate of 0.1. Their shredded shells are downgraded into such things as carpet tuft and jacket liner. Bottles cannot be reused because polymers are not sterilisable, nor can they be 'genuinely' recycled into more bottles for hygiene reasons. **[576]** RM/British Plastics Federation. Based on an average 34,000 bottles per ton. A negligible number is recycled or reused. **[577]** RM/*Canada Yearbook* (1992). An expanse of 2,206,000 km, which appear a lot, until you find out that long leases on huge areas are handed out to corporations. Many were given free in the 1950s. Mexico fits comfortably into them with room to spare. The official forestry industry slogan is 'Forests Forever', but felled original forests are replaced not by forests, but by monoculture plantations dangerously susceptible to pest infection, requiring massive chemical and other treatments. Selective logging by resident wardens and slashed paper use are the only eco-future. **[578]** *Earth First! Reader*. Virgin areas of Washington and Oregon are due for 30,000 miles of roads. Virgin areas of Montana, Idaho, Wyoming, Utah, Nevada, Colorado, Arizona and New Mexico are due for 33,000. The US Forest Service and US Bureau of 'Land Management' log eight sq miles of old-growth forest per month in Oregon alone. The logging roads are heavily subsidised by the taxpayer, effectively contributing to paper and pulp corporations' profits. Hypnotised wilderness wreckers in the industry call environmentalists 'tree-huggers'. **[579]** RM/*Canada Yearbook* (1992). A year's tree planting in Quebec, BC and Ontario (700m in 1990) would have put 53 trees on each burned football field of forest, leaving none for logged-off areas. Facts like that make observers highly sceptical of the 'Forests Forever' slogan of the Canadian industry that supplies so much of British paper-based products. Fire is one of the four elements of Earth, brought by lightning and naturally regenerating tree life. **[580]** RM/Statistical Abstract of the US. A total of 1.35m acres, or an area 30 per cent larger than the county of Hampshire. **[581]** RM/OECD. From 754m (1970) to 731m (1987), or from 96 Switzerlands to 93. **[582]** *Canada Yearbook* (1992). The next year (1988–9) the take was down 42 per cent to 267,427. **[583]** *Canada Yearbook* (1992). The following year they were down to 41,998. **[584]** *Canada Yearbook* (1992). **[585]** *Canada Yearbook* (1992). **[586]** OECD. Thirty per cent of Western Europe's glass gets recycled – only 17 per cent in the UK. One of the biggest problems is the mixture of glass colours. Another is plunging prices of cullet (scrap glass) as consumers respond to recycling appeals. The locally circulated returnable container is the only ecological future. **[587]** Dept of the Environment (22 Oct 1990). **[588]** Dept of the Environment (Hansard, 22 October 1990). Germany and the Netherlands' per capita recycling of glass is reckoned to be three to five times as good as Great Britain's. Mixed glass colours are hampering the recycling effort, and prices have fluctuated badly. The British beer bottle is to turn green, because of the volume of imported green wine bottles recycled. The only eco-future is locally-filled returnable containers and/or refill packs. **[589]** *The Economist* (1990). A total of ECU2,000,000. MEPs appear to do a lot of shuttling between

Strasbourg and Brussels. **[590]** HM Treasury (1990). **[591]** Home Office
(1990). **[592]** *Lloyds List*. **[593]** *Lloyds List*. A classic example of the
delirious growth dreams in Europe's corporate boardrooms. Three per
cent growth a year doubles turnover in 23 years. Even if this were
sustainable for one generation, or two, it is clearly unsustainable on a
long-term basis. **[593a]** Environmental Protection Agency. US reporting
producers released 11.2m tons of toxic chemicals in 1987 (the latest
year), according to the US EPA. **[594]** Economist Intelligence Unit.
Canada's figure is 7.1 (*Canada Yearbook*, 1992), but in predominantly
native-populated North West Territories it is 16.2. In Mexico the rate is 47
(*UN Demographic Yearbook*, 1989). **[595]** Economist Intelligence Unit.
[596] RM/Euromonitor. Total annual cigarettes smoked in Europe, Scandinavia and the former Soviet Union is 1,361,395m (1990). **[597]** *Quid*
(1989). **[598]** BBC (1992). Estimates put the female rate at 1:800. But
could HIV not be the cause of AIDS? Dissident virologists point to AIDS
victims being 90 per cent male, while virus infections normally do not
discriminate between the sexes. They also note that billions of dollars
worth of research have not succeeded in predicting exactly what sickness the HIV carrier will die of. Some ascribe the blame for AIDS to other
causes, among them drug abuse and AZT, the AIDS treatment. **[599]**
Economist Intelligence Unit. **[600]** Economist Intelligence Unit. **[601]** *The
Lancet* (1992). **[602]** *Time*. Greater than the population of Venezuela.
[603] *The Lancet*. Britain's NHS is exactly that: a public service, available
to all. **[604]** *The Economist* (1990). The life expectancy of US Hispanic
seasonal and migrant farmworkers is 49 years (National Migrant
Resource Program Inc [1990]). **[605]** RM/Euromonitor. **[606]** OECD
(1988). **[607]** OECD. It may seem surprising that the USA has fewer
doctors for its population than Spain. **[608]** Dr Aleksei V. Yablokov. **[609]**
US Bureau of Indian Affairs (1987)/*Canada Yearbook* (1992). There are
861,500 living on or near US reservations (total native population 1.5m);
60 per cent of Canada's 466,440 status Indians living on reserves the
size of Haiti in total. All native peoples' vital statistics have improved
considerably over the last two decades, although deaths per 1,000 live
births in the predominantly aboriginal North West Territories are 16.2,
compared with a national Canadian rate of 7.1. **[610]** DTI (1990). **[611]**
DTI. Given the acknowledged difference in measurement of data
between EC countries, Germany's research and development figure
showing nearly three times greater expenditure is surprising. **[612]**
Eurostat/RM. **[613]** Predicast/Imp&Tractr. Some 1.1m riding lawn-
mowers are sold a year, and this calculation averages their cut at 4ft,
mowing 10 acres a day. In addition, 5.7m non-riding power lawn-mowers
are shipped each year. **[614]** D. Icke, *It Doesn't Have To Be Like This*.
[615] D. Icke, *It Doesn't Have To Be Like This*. **[616]** *Statistical Abstract of
the US* (1989). Three 18-wheelers of gold were mined in 1984 (2m fine
oz), and increased by 365 per cent in 1989 to 7.6m fine oz. **[617]** *The

Futurist. **[618]** EPA. Dioxins are emitted by garbage incinerators. Eskimo breast milk has been shown to be 17 times more traced with effluent poisons than that of North American urban mothers. **[619]** RM/Euromonitor (1989). A total of $216m per year. **[620]** RM/Euromonitor (1989). A total of $93m per year. **[621]** OECD. **[622]** OECD. Americans emitted 89.2 kg per capita in 1970, 80.4 in 1988. Japanese issued 15.9 kgs in 1970; 9.7 in 1986, nearly one-tenth as much. Nitrogen oxides increase human susceptibility to viruses, irritate the lungs, cause bronchitis and pneumonia and may be linked with increasing hay fever. **[623]** *Time.* **[624]** Dept of Energy. **[625]** UNCED 1992, *United States of America Report.* **[626]** Dr Aleksei V. Yablokov. **[627]** RM/Euromonitor/*The Economist.* A swap of all atmosphere-wrecking domestic fridges in Europe will cost some £42bn. **[628]** Alex Kirby, BBC Radio News. **[629]** William C. Burns, *Information Please Almanac.* **[630]** RM/*Canada Yearbook* (1992). Montreal to Houston and back. (8.8m tons in 1991.) Between 10 and 17 trees are needed to produce a ton of paper, or enough for around 7,000 copies of a national newspaper. To produce 400,000 copies of *The Independent on Sunday* requires the felling of between 570 and 969 trees every week. The trees are supposed to be cropped like corn on a sustainable basis, but there is furious controversy over whether they actually are. **[631]** RM/*Canada Yearbook* (1992). Twenty-five tons in 1991. Only 800 miles short of Capetown-to-London. Bleaching pulp to produce white paper products requires extremely powerful chemical agents with polluting side-products. Off-white or light brown unbleached products cause much less pollution. **[632]** OECD. Twenty-five per cent of waste paper is recycled in the US, up from 19 per cent in 1975. But 50 per cent is recycled in Japan, and 40–45 per cent in Western Europe where per capita consumption is lower, being about 165 kg in the UK (*Warmer Bulletin*), 200 kg in Germany, 110 kg in Italy. **[633]** RM/Euromonitor (1990). A total of $72m per year. **[634]** RM/Euromonitor (1990). An amount of $591m per year. Most environmental health laws forbid the deposit of excrement in waste, yet this obvious hygiene requirement is ignored everywhere. Clearly there is a danger of coliform bacteria leaching into water supplies and such cases are, indeed, cropping up. So-called disposables have been shown not to be disposable at all, because they remain undegraded in landfill for decades. **[635]** Lord President of the Council. **[636]** Lord President of the Council. **[637]** Graef S. Crystal. **[638]** Graef S. Crystal. Extrapolated from his 1990 annual salary of $11.5m at four per cent. **[639]** *Spy.* 1991 figure. This exceptional figure is included because it must be a corporate record-breaker. About £43m. **[640]** Goskompriroda, cited in *Worldwatch Paper 99.* **[641]** Agrow. Pesticides were originally developed from chemical weapons made during the Second World War. Their main function is as an aid to the mechanisation of farming. **[642]** Barry Commoner. Stretching from Boston to Calgary and back: 250m lbs. Agrichem companies are selling US farming corporations an integrated package of fake fertility for sponge-like soil, a totally poisoned environment, and plant breeds genetically engineered to be impervious to either. This ghastly vision is already taking shape in the cotton plantations. Florida is now taking the vision yet further by using nuclear irradiation on the fruits of such wastelands so that they are devoid of life-giving rot. **[643]** RM/*Le Monde*. Based on FF5.50 per litre at FF10 to the £1. **[644]** RM/*USA Today*. One of the prime reasons for the USA's impending collision with the global warming crisis is its incapability of pricing (which means mostly taxing) oil energy in line with the rest of the world. In real terms, the price of gasoline has actually gone down by 4 per cent since the 1950s. **[645]** OECD. This figure shows the course EC consumption is steering by. An emerging response to the plastics torrent is incineration, but many plastics release toxins on incineration. Ecologists argue that locally reused containers are the only sustainable way forward, at least in the field of food and drink packaging. Plastic containers are unsterilisable after use. **[646]** OECD. Some 26m tonnes of plastics were consumed in Europe in 1989, a figure rising every year. An average European family of four throws away around 40kg of plastic each year. Plastics occupy 20–30 per cent of household waste bags – about seven per cent by weight. Half the plastics purchased by householders are packaging materials. Consultants Landbank Trust consider plastics to be fundamentally unsuited to a recycling economy because of the six basic polymers (and dozens of others) used. **[647]** OECD. **[648]** Dept of the Environment (1990). Some 3,000 have been treated with lime in an effort to revive life. British sulphur emissions from power stations like Drax in Yorkshire are the culprits. Hundreds of millions are now being spent on scrubbers for Drax (but the global warming emissions remain). **[649]** OECD (1985). This figure, 0.3 per cent in 1972 (EPA) is expected to rise to 2.8 per cent in 2000 by the US Environmental Protection Agency. But it will probably rise faster, and environmental defence will overtake military defence (5.5 per cent of GNP in 1990 [Economist Intelligence Unit]). **[650]** OECD (1985). **[651]** OECD (1986). Canadians emitted about 176 kg of sulphur dioxide in 1980, which has now been reduced by 40 per cent. But Canada still receives 3.5m to 4m tons per year of atmospheric SO2 from the USA. **[652]** RM/Eurostat. A total of 4,383 people (car occupancy 5), and a tailback of cars 1.6m long. Forty-eight million added 1960–90. **[653]** US Bureau of the Census. US population increase since 1980 is greater than the population of Venezuela. Official annual percentage population increase has slowed steadily since the 1950s (1.7) and 1960s (1.3), through the 1970s (1.1) to the 1980s (0.9) but, as the total grows, declining percentage increases are misleading. Recent figures may underrate illegal immigration, even after amnesties. Pacific seaboard states' populations increased at twice the national rate in the 1980s, by 23 per cent. **[654]** RM/Euromonitor. 51,576 miles. Canada lost 1,344 miles of track between 1986 and 1988. **[655]** Dept of Transport (1990). **[656]** Dept of Transport (1990). **[657]** Dept of Transport (1990). **[658]** EPA. This shows how garbage can be reduced at the stroke of a pen, like Boris Yeltsin abolishing the Communist Party. Bring back the bring-back! **[659]** *Time*. **[660]** *Worldwatch Paper 99*. Populous cities such as Kaunas, Luthuania and Riga, capital of Latvia, do not have any sewage treatment facilities, according to the Worldwatch Institute (1990). Remember that 53 per cent of Scottish sewage is untreated. Much British sewage is emitted untreated during rainstorms. **[661]** Council on Environmental Quality. This does not refer to people with septic tanks or soakaways. It means people whose mains drainage either pours away (into rivers or bays) untreated or is crudely screened in non-storm conditions. **[662]** RM/Euromonitor. London to Brighton, every year. That telltale pink adhesive pantyliner strip protector is visible all over Europe's beaches and riverbanks. Historically, women made use of strips of waste fabric, or washed and reused napkins. The idea of buying 139,000 tons of high-tech, chlorine-bleached products a year, risking toxic shock syndrome, was unimaginable. **[663]** Euromonitor/RM. Counting a shopping mall as 10 acres, they would fill the city of San Francisco 15 times over. **[664]** *Worldwatch Paper 99*. A total of at least 1.5bn tons. **[665]** *Statistical Abstract of the US*. Not far short of the human numbers in Bangladesh. The methane from their bowels makes a significant contribution to greenhouse gases. In the USA: 99m, 12.3m in Canada. Cattle are also a very inefficient way to turn sunlight into protein. **[666]** *The Lancet*. The doctor's oath to preserve life becomes an ethical maze when medical technology can preserve half-life and bodies functioning with dead front brains. **[667]** OECD (1986). The Japanese already had one-third the per capita emissions of Americans in 1970. After a determined clean-up they have one-twelfth. While the USA reduced emissions during 1980 to 1988 by 24 per cent, New York only managed 13 per cent. National performance on nitrogen dioxide reduction was even worse: only nine per cent over the same period. **[668]** RM/Dr Volker Beer, cited in *Worldwatch Paper 99* (1990). SO2 pollution, and acid rain, are a serious problem in Central Europe, resulting from burning of lignite coal at such plants. In industrial areas of Central Europe, average annual airborne sulphur dioxide levels are often five times the USA standard, the Worldwatch Institute reports. Nevertheless, emissions per capita in the US remain higher than those of Romania. Former East Germans emitted a record 317 kilos of SO2, compared with 64 in the United Kingdom; Czechs, 179 kilos (UN 1990). **[669]** Neil Postman, *Entertaining Ourselves to Death*. A total of 56,000 items in four years. **[670]** MITI. This date shows how close the consumer electronics age was when the Wall Street collapse of 1929, the ensuing Great Depression and World War deferred it for 30 years. **[671]** *The Timetables of History*. **[672]** *The Timetables of History*. **[673]** *Campaign*. **[674]** Predicast/*Fortune* (1991). How many are necessary?

[675] Foreign and Commonwealth Office. **[676]** French Tourist Office. When does a religious shrine become a tourist shrine, and what is a tourist shrine? What is tourism? The new 'generation' of jumbo jets is being built to carry 600 tourists at a time. But will tourist air traffic survive the ozone-layer shock, after airline corporations become unable any longer to hide the secret that their planes spew chlorine compounds into the upper atmosphere? **[677]** David Nicholson-Lord. **[678]** David Nicholson-Lord. **[679]** David Nicholson-Lord. This projected figure is symptomatic of the current fossil-fuel fantasia. Who are the idealists? Those who dream of nearly a billion tourists on the shores of the Med in the summer season? Or those who say it is a dangerous delusion? **[680]** OECD/EPA. Meadows, Meadows and Jorgen in *Beyond The Limits To Growth*: 'A total of 65,000 industrial chemicals are now in regular use. Toxicology data are available on fewer than one per cent of them. Every day three to five new chemicals enter the marketplace. Eighty per cent of these chemicals are not tested for toxicity. Every day 1m tons of hazardous wastes are generated in the world, 90 per cent of them in the industrialised world.' **[681]** RM/Predicast/Environmental Science. 1991 total 265m tons, 10-hr average day. Canada adds another two/three miles. In North America a year's hazardous wastes would stretch 123,000 miles, or from Prudhoe Bay to Tierra Del Fuego and back four times. **[682]** MAFF. The EC Commission's vision of a mega-market interlaced with superhighways along which fly fuel-guzzling juggernauts carrying identical produce is an accounting lunacy underwritten by energy illiteracy and waste blindness. No people in their right minds would bank all their food, shelter and livelihood on fuels obtained thousands of miles away from uncertain allies – and yet such is precisely the long-term EC project. Whom is the idealist? Those who envisage self-sufficiency in poultry? Or those who rely on imports from across a continent? **[683]** DTI (1989). **[684]** DTI (1989). **[685]** Dept of Transport. **[686]** Dept of Transport. **[687]** Euromonitor/RM. Most of the fuel is imported to EC states. When it burns, precious life-giving oxygen is used up and greenhouse-effect carbon dioxide is released. **[688]** Economist Intelligence Unit. Jet aircraft emit ozone-eating gases into the upper atmosphere, and in certain conditions their condensation trails reduce ground-level sunlight. Their fuel greed is enormous, and they are getting slower – congestion and delays at airports are notorious. In Europe, high-speed trains are a growing alternative, sometimes matching speeds door-to-door on short hauls, with much better fuel efficiency. When the ozone-layer crisis hits the USA, air travel may have to be reduced or eliminated. Hi-speed trains are being planned in the USA. **[689]** RM/Economist Intelligence Unit. In 1988 vehicle/km for cars was 2,316bn, for buses 9bn. Yet for commuting (5–50 km), buses (at 56 occupancy) are more than 10 times more efficient than cars (occupancy 1) in carbon dioxide emissions per person. Even for local shopping (2–5 km), buses (at 25 occupancy) are more than twice as efficient as cars (occupancy 2) [Friends of the Earth]. This consideration will become increasingly urgent as legislators struggle to meet worldwide carbon-dioxide cuts. **[690]** Economist Intelligence Unit. **[691]** RM/Economist Intelligence Unit. Fuel-efficiency taxes will cause merchandisers to seek shorter hauls. Decentralisation will become a market force, and truck mileage will shrink. **[692]** RM/US Dept of Statistics/Gas Facts. **[693]** RM/*Journal of the American Planning Association*, cited in *Worldwatch Paper 99*. Averaged from Poland (85), Hungary (58), Czechoslovakia (52) and East Germany (27). (Figures 1990.) The UK figure is 19. The USA, 3. The rush to car ownership promises to change this situation. **[694]** RM/Economist Intelligence Unit. This scale of increase, from 2,768bn to 3,259bn, will have to be reversed in coming years, as carbon dioxide emission cuts begin to bite. **[695]** RM/Motor Vehicle Manufacturers' Assoc. of the US. Canada pro rata 10 per cent. World car, truck and bus population is estimated at 556,931,000 (1989), which, extrapolated conservatively at three per cent a year, gives 608m for 1992. A three per cent annual growth rate would double production to 1.1bn a year in 2000. **[696]** Dept of Transport (1990). **[697]** Dept of Transport (1990). **[698]** HM Monopolies and Mergers Commission. **[699]** HM Monopolies and Mergers Commission. **[700]** *The Economist*. **[701]** *New Statesman & Society* (1992). **[702]** Alan Clarke, MP (1992, pro-rated from 1990 at five per cent). **[703]** Ministry of Defence. **[704]** *Jane's Fighting Ships*. **[705]** RM/Predicast/Environmental Science. 1991 US total 163m tons, 10-hour average day. Canada extrapolated at 10 per cent. Some pious aims have been expressed recently, because of the mounting landfill crisis. Canada aims to cut landfill waste by 50 per cent by 2000. Even if both the US and Canada achieved that goal, about 38,000 miles of nose-to-tail 18-wheelers would still be lining up at landfills every year. There is no realistic solution except the one business will not face: reduced consumption, radical decentralisation, energy cuts. **[706]** RM/*The Independent*. London to Naples as the crow flies. **[707]** RM/Euromonitor. Shaving with the water running uses between 10 and 15 gallons of heated drinking water. **[708]** EPA (1991). Recycling can help, too – Seattle has a current rate of 34 per cent, aiming for 60 per cent by 1998. But the elimination of planned obsolescence, drastic cuts in packaging, radical changes in transportation and distribution and, above all, product repair and re-use, are the only non-addictive strategies. **[709]** Clarke, de Kadt, Saphire, *Burning Garbage in the US*/Inform. Some 5.5m tons per year. The authors note 'there is a lack of clear guidance from the EPA on appropriate control and treatment for disposal or reuse of these residues', which is unsurprising, since the ash contains many toxic residues and heavy metals. Only six per cent of UK rubbish is currently incinerated, but landfill sites are running out and recycling is looking increasingly expensive for industry. Pressure to match high northern EC incineration rates will grow. **[710]** Office of Technology Assessment.

Extrapolated from a 1989 figure of $500bn. It accounts for federal primary and secondary education programmes budgets from 1993 to 2019. The salaries would populate Canada. **[711]** RM/Environmental Action. From New York to Tampa. **[712]** Euromonitor/RM. Flushing a toilet takes between four and seven gallons of drinking water. **[713]** RM/British Plastics Federation. Calculated on the basis of an average 34,000 bottles per ton, or 2.2m tons a year. The juggernauts would stretch about 968 miles nose-to-tail. **[714]** *Worldwatch Paper 99* (1990). **[715]** *Worldwatch Paper 99* (1990). **[716]** Czech radio reports, cited in *Worldwatch Paper 99* (1990). Eighty per cent of a 40,000 ton a year total. **[717]** *British Medical Journal.* **[718]** RM/Eurostat. Over half a million a year. The number of children affected is unknown. It is very rare for parents to divorce with the consent of their children. Thus a concern for the rights of children would indicate much stricter restrictions on divorce. **[719]** WHO/*British Medical Journal.* **[720]** Graef S. Crystal. **[721]** *Fairness and Accuracy in Reporting* (1989). Seventy per cent of world business is done by transnational corporations, the great majority of which are based in the USA, and which heavily influence news content through their dominance of television production income by advertising budgets. All transnationals are constructed on a basis of at least three per cent growth per annum, a rate which doubles production of turnover in 23 years. **[722]** *Forbes.* Kluge gambled up a small fortune while gaining an economics degree at Columbia University, USA, in the 1930s. After serving in US military intelligence, he bought a radio station in Maryland and formed Metromedia, a media conglomerate. He also owns a 10,000-acre estate in Vermont, USA, where Forbes reports his third ex-wife owning 9.7 acres. Forbes counts Kluge as America's richest man.

SOUTHERN HEMISPHERE ZONE [723] Royal Mail International. **[724]** World Society for the Protection of Animals. **[725]** World Society for the Protection of Animals. **[726]** The US Commission on Integrated Long-Term Strategy. This is a predicted increase from $240bn in 1990 at 1986 constant dollars, or 3.25 times. **[727]** The US Commission on Integrated Long-Term Strategy. Up from $42bn in 1990 in 1986 constant dollars. **[728]** Royal Mail International. **[729]** Royal Mail International. In the USA, the figure drops to 1.8 people per car. **[730]** United Nations (1992). **[731]** Girardet, Herbert: *Earthrise.* Girardet considers Lagos to have the world's highest room occupancy rate. The city also reflects Nigeria's daunting population problem, with a population growing at six per cent a year. Using Dr David Suzuki's exponential growth formula of dividing 70 by the annual growth percentage to find the doubling period, that gives 17 years before Lagos's size doubles. **[732]** *The Economist* (1987). **[733]** *The Economist* (1987). A Canadian's was 9,915. **[734]** *The Economist* (1987). An Australian's was 6,845. **[735]** Royal Mail International. Japan has 26 times greater commercial vehicle production than India, with one-fifth the population. **[736]** Royal Mail International. **[737]** *The Economist*. **[738]** Hutchinson. **[739]** Hutchinson. **[740]** Siemens. **[741]** Siemens. **[742]** Royal Mail International. **[743]** Royal Mail International. **[744]** *Time* (1991). **[745]** *The Economist* **[746]** ISS (1980). **[747]** *New Internationalist*. **[748]** *New Internationalist*. **[749]** Euromonitor. **[750]** Euromonitor. **[751]** E. Goldsmith and N. Hildyard, *The Social and Environmental Impact of Large Dams* (1984). **[752]** E. Goldsmith and N. Hildyard, *The Social and Environmental Impact of Large Dams* (1984). **[753]** Probe International. **[754]** Probe International. **[755]** *The Ecologist*. **[756]** Probe International (1991). **[757]** Probe International. **[758]** Probe International. **[759]** UNCED (1990). **[760]** *New Statesman & Society*. **[761]** Worldwatch Institute: *State of the World* (1989). **[762]** Probe International. **[763]** Knight-Ridder *Tribune News*. **[764]** Knight-Ridder *Tribune News*. **[765]** E. Goldsmith and N. Hildyard, *The Social and Environmental Impact of Large Dams* (1984). **[766]** E. Goldsmith and N. Hildyard, *The Social and Environmental Impact of Large Dams* (1984). **[767]** Heinemann Philip. **[768]** Heinemann Philip. **[769]** I.G. Simmons, *Changing the Face of The Earth*, cited in Herbert Girardet, *Earthrise*. Astronauts consume about 2.74m kcal per day. **[770]** I.G. Simmons, *Changing the Face of The Earth*, cited in Herbert Girardet, *Earthrise*. For thousands of years, hunter-gatherers in the forests that covered 90 per cent of the planet used less, about 2,000 k/cal. **[771]** World Resources/RM. An area of 565 hectares. **[772]** World Resources/RM. An area of 5,769 hectares. **[773]** *State of the World Report* (1990). An area of 59m hectares. **[774]** *State of the World Report* (1990). An area of 19m hectares. **[775]** *The Economist*. **[776]** RM/Dept of Health (1990). **[777]** Dept of Education. **[778]** Dept of Education. **[779]** Royal Mail International. **[780]** Royal Mail International. **[781]** World Resources Institute. **[782]** OECD. **[783]** *The Futurist* (May/June 1992). **[784]** *The Gaia Atlas of Planet Management*. **[785]** *The Gaia Atlas of Planet Management*. **[786]** *New State of the World Atlas* (1989). **[787]** *New State of the World Atlas* (1989). **[788]** *New State of the World Atlas* (1989). **[789]** *New State of the World Atlas* (1989). **[790]** *New State of the World Atlas* (1989). **[791]** *New State of the World Atlas* (1989). **[792]** Probe International. **[793]** Mustafa K. Tolba, *Saving Our Planet*. Of them 10.5m are children under five. In developed countries, the figure is about 500,000. **[794]** *The Economist*. **[795]** RM/Euromonitor (1990). **[796]** RM/Euromonitor. **[797]** *UN World Economic Survey* (1991). **[798]** C.M. Becker, *World Development Report* (1990). **[799]** C.M. Becker, *World Development Report* (1990). **[800]** The Vatican (1991). **[801]** The Vatican (1991). **[802]** *The Futurist* (May/June 1992). **[803]** ECLAC. **[804]** Mustafa K. Tolba, *Saving Our Planet*. **[805]** *New State of the World Atlas* (1987). **[806]** *New State of the World Atlas* (1987). **[807]** *New State of the World Atlas* (1987). **[808]** *New State of the World Atlas* (1987). **[809]** Royal Mail International. **[810]** Probe International. **[811]** Royal Mail International. **[812]** Royal Mail International. **[813]**

Mustafa K. Tolba, *Saving Our Planet*. International tourist receipts were put at about $300bn in 1990. Build Bali in your own back yard! **[814]** Royal Mail International. Inflated by religious visits to Mecca. **[815]** RM/Christy Campbell. A total of 955,044 tons. **[816]** RM/BBC TV. A 54-day campaign, with 20,000 tons of bombs dropped per day, as announced by the high command on 9 February 1991. The calculation gives a total bombardment greater than that delivered by the RAF against Nazi Germany. The Pentagon has subsequently admitted what it at first furiously denied, that the destruction of Iraq's civil power supplies cut the population's water off and unleashed a major typhoid epidemic that may have killed as many as 350,000 children (Harvard Medical Team). **[817]** UN World Economic Survey (1991).

COMMAND CENTRE [818] J. Ehrlichman, *The Guardian*, cited in Lang and Clutterbuck, *P Is For Pesticides* (1991). (1992 extrapolated at 4 per cent from estimated $21.5bn in 1989.) In the 25 years to 1983, world sales grew at an average 12.5 per cent a year, the authors report. **[819]** FAO. **[820]** FAO. **[821]** BBC/Helen Sharman. In one of the last Soviet orbital flights. **[822]** Al Gore, *Earth In The Balance*. **[823]** DRI. **[824]** Frankfurt '91 Motor Fair. **[825]** Frankfurt '91 Motor Fair (1990). **[826]** Al Gore, *Earth In The Balance*. **[827]** WHO. **[828]** Mustafa K. Tolba, *Saving Our Planet*. Up from 200m in 1970. The figures clearly reflect the corresponding figures for depopulation of the world's countryside; from 62.9 per cent of the population in 1970 to 57.4 per cent in 1990, towards an expected 40 per cent in 2025. **[829]** A. Milne, *Our Drowning World*. This periodicity has prompted the question: do ice and water ages occur at 20,000-year intervals? **[830]** A. Milne, *Our Drowning World*. Milne asks: Larger than Europe, could the Antarctic sheet detach from terra firma and shift? **[831]** A. Milne, *Our Drowning World*. Milne asks: Antarctica has melted and refrozen for 7,000 years – will it go on? **[832]** NASA/ BBC. **[833]** *Life*. **[834]** *Life*. **[835]** Dr Richard Haines. **[836]** Denys Trussell (1992 gross estimate from official sources). **[837]** RM/E. Goldsmith and N. Hildyard, *The Social and Environmental Impact of Large Dams* (1984). **[838]** Goldsmith and Hildyard, *The Social and Environmental Impact of Large Dams* (1984). The authors point out that such expanses of restrained water are the only works of man visible on a satellite view of the world. **[839]** RM/Goldsmith and Hildyard, *The Social and Environmental Impact of Large Dams* (1984). **[840]** RM/Goldsmith and Hildyard, *The Social and Environmental Impact of Large Dams* (1984) est 1990. Thirteen hundred terawatt-hours were produced on the world's rivers in 1984. **[841]** Goldsmith and Hildyard, *The Social and Environmental Impact of Large Dams* (1984)/T.W. Mermel. **[842]** Goldsmith and Hildyard, *The Social and Environmental Impact of Large Dams* (1984). **[843]** *National Geographic*. **[844]** *Whole Earth Review*. The carbon dioxide is saved in reduced demand for electrical power stations, most of which burn fossil fuels. **[845]** Dr David Suzuki, *Inventing The Future*. Four per cent growth gives the sum 70 divided by four = 17.5 years to double; five per cent gives the sum 70 divided by 5 = 14 years; six per cent, 11.5 years and so on. **[846]** RM/Richard North, *The Real Cost*. Eight billion hectares. **[847]** *The Ecologist* (calculated on the basis of 10 kilocalories of fossil fuel energy for one calorie of edible food). **[848]** R.P. Ambroggi, *Scientific American*. **[849]** R.P. Ambroggi, *Scientific American*. **[850]** R.P. Ambroggi, *Scientific American*. **[851]** President George Bush, 24 Feb 1992. **[852]** *The Ecologist* (Sept/Oct 1991). This figure, from German sources published in Stockholm, refers to small-scale field tests, but any release into the environment of genetic structures that have been tinkered with represents a gamble that few people under family or community circumstances would care to take. Only the machine-like organisational rationale of transnational corporations makes such risks seem acceptable to those involved. **[853]** *Chemical and Engineering News* (11 March 1991). In spite of the huge proliferation of pesticides, many of them transgenic, it is common knowledge that pest damage remains unabated and in some sectors is actually on the increase. **[854]** G.P. Geoghian, cited in *The Ecologist* (Sept/Oct 1991). **[855]** *Time/Life*. **[856]** *USA Today*. Enough to populate the city of Augusta, Georgia, USA. **[857]** The Global Tomorrow Coalition. **[858]** UK Milk Marketing Board. **[859]** Al Gore, *Earth In The Balance*. Twenty-three per cent is carbon, 2.6 per cent nitrogen, 1.4 per cent calcium, 1.1 per cent phosphorus and about three dozen other elements. **[860]** *Time*. **[861]** University of Calgary, Canada. **[862]** RM. Years spent in a hypnotic trance? **[863]** RM/Prof. Victor Kovda, University of Moscow (1990 est). A total of 250m hectares, put at 180m in the early 1970s, 250m by 2001. Irrigation has been associated with severe salination problems, potentially resulting in desertification. **[864]** *Quid* (1989). **[865]** *Quid* (1989). **[866]** Richard North, *The Real Cost*. **[867]** International Soil Reference and Information Centre, Wageningen, Netherlands, cited by Mustafa K. Tolba, *Saving Our Planet*. **[868]** RM/Richard North, *The Real Cost*. Equivalent to 1.5 hectares. When Richard North wrote his book in 1981, there were five arable acres per person. Population increase has reduced the share. **[869]** UNEP. **[870]** UNEP. **[871]** ITOPF and Lloyd's Maritime Information service. A total of 15,000,000 bbls. **[872]** Meadows, Meadows and Randers, *Beyond The Limits*. About 2bn tons, or nose-to-tail semi-trailer trucks stretching 860,881 miles, or to the Moon 3.6 times. **[873]** Hall, Cleveland and Kaufmann, *Energy and Resource Quality* (1986). **[874]** R. Body. **[875]** Zed Books/RM. **[876]** Meadows, Meadows and Randers, *Beyond The Limits*. Reserves, yes, but not oil that can be burned in the biosphere without great risk to the climate. Anyway, what about the next 50,000 years of our species? What will be their supply? Even the wildest estimates of undiscovered reserves only double the amount, and we have already used nearly a fifth of it! **[877]** Meadows,

Meadows and Randers, *Beyond The Limits.* **[878]** Carl Sagan, cited in *Earth Conference One/In Context* magazine. **[879]** RM/*Gaia Atlas of the World.* **[880]** *National Geographic,* Spring 1992. **[881]** FAO. **[882]** Al Gore, *Earth In The Balance*, citing Russian environmentalist Alexei Yablokov. **[883]** Agrow, 11 Aug 1989, cited in *Worldwatch Paper 99.* Every year 700,000 illnesses are attributed to pesticides. **[884]** Al Gore, *Earth In The Balance.* Meadows, Meadows and Randers in *Beyond The Limits* add that Stanford University researchers found humans commandeering 25 per cent of the total photosynthetic energy of earth, land and sea. **[885]** *New York Times.* **[886]** UN Economic Commission for Europe (1989), cited in *Worldwatch Paper 99.* Poland possesses Europe's largest virgin forest, covering some 308,750 acres. **[887]** Population Institute, Washington, DC. Fewer than 2m Americans were born in the same year. **[888]** Population Institute, Washington, DC. Computer modelled, census-based. **[889]** Mustafa K. Tolba, *Saving Our Planet.* Poor people overall in developing countries are estimated at 1,116m, promising to rise to 1,300m by 2000 and 1,500m by 2025. **[890]** Al Gore, *Earth In The Balance.* Some 250m tribal people still live in traditional pre-industrial ways the world over. **[891]** SustainAbility (2–3bn barrels). **[892]** Robert A. Egli, Office for Chemistry of the Atmosphere, Schaffhausen, Switzerland (1990); with thanks to Olaf Achilles. 'The 176m tons of air-traffic fuel burned in 1990 produced about 550m tons of CO_2, 220m tons of water, 3.5m tons of NOX, and 180,000 tons of sulphur dioxide. . . . Regular subsonic air traffic is responsible for a 10 per cent increase in the nitric acid concentration at 21 km above sea level, one of the most critical altitudes for ozone holes. What do you think, reader? Considering they may be playing an important part in destroying Earth, should jets fly on? **[893]** *In Context* magazine. Half of the world's reactors are on, or under, the sea. **[894]** Royal Aircraft Establishment. *In Context* magazine reports that scientists have looked at only 10 per cent of all the data sent back to Earth by satellites in orbit, and have closely analysed no more than 1 per cent, citing *Worldwatch Magazine* (Sept/Oct 89). **[895]** Mustafa K. Tolba, *Saving Our Planet.* **[896]** *State of the World Report* (1990). Calculated by the excess of soil loss over new soil naturally arising. **[897]** *The Ecologist.* Accelerated soil erosion occurs as a result of land clearance and farm mechanisation. For example, earth washed off the deforested Himalayas can clearly be seen by satellite being washed hundreds of miles into the Bay of Bengal. *National Geographic* has published revealing photographs of the soil loss around the coasts of Madagascar. Washington's Worldwatch Institute considers this widely ignored phenomenon to be a serious long-term problem for world agriculture. **[898]** RM/Richard North, *The Real Cost.* **[899]** John Lichfield. **[900]** AT&T **[901]** P. Chapman, *Fuels Paradise.* **[902]** E. Goldsmith, *The Way.* Edward Goldsmith anticipates that humanity intends to use 100 per cent of the biosphere's net primary production each year. **[903]** RM/Euromonitor. **[904]** *Nature* (10

Oct 1991). **[905]** OECD. **[906]** UK Home office. **[907]** World Resources (1988–9). **[908]** RM/Ruth Leger Sivard/Global Tomorrow Coalition. **[909]** Hutchinson. **[910]** Hutchinson. **[911]** Michael Renner, World Watch Institute. An authoritative survey has predicted 2m extra cancer deaths in the long-term as a result of atmospheric nuclear testing. France, a detonator of huge devices over Mururoa Atoll in the Pacific Ocean for three decades, announced a one-year moratorium in April 1992. **[912]** Jeremy Rifkin, *Biosphere Politics.* **[913]** Sivard, *World Military and Social Expenditures.* **[914]** A. Milne, *Our Drowning World.* **[915]** A. Milne, *Our Drowning World.* **[916]** A. Milne, *Our Drowning World.* **[917]** A. Milne, *Our Drowning World.* **[918]** Labour Party, *An Earthly Chance.* One second of world waste would fill 45 semi-trailer trucks. **[919]** RM/*Atlas of the Environment.* Junked tackle represents a major hazard for marine species. **[920]** RM/*Atlas of the Environment.* **[921]** McDonald's. This number has become a little legend of the packaging world. It is the original of dozens of others that have followed from the massive waste-generating machine that is America's fast-food empire. **[922]** Mustafa K. Tolba, *Saving Our Planet.* **[923]** UNEP. **[924]** Milos Holy, Czech section, International Committee on Large Dams. Opinions vary on these huge estimates. This one is 1,400bn. **[925]** Rm/E. Goldsmith and N. Hildyard, *The Social and Environmental Impact of Large Dams* (1984). 100,000 cu km, 30–40 per cent of which goes into the sea.

HUMAN FACTORS [926] Germain, *Reproductive Health and Dignity.* **[927]** Germain, *Reproductive Health and Dignity.* **[928]** WHO/Worldwatch Institute. **[929]** Worldwatch Institute. Compared with 6m live births. Other unofficial estimates put the number of Soviet Union abortions at between 11m and 20m. **[930]** Euromonitor. **[931]** Population Institute, Washington, DC. Number of babies: 1,637. **[932]** Population Institute, Washington, DC. An increase of 140m carloads (702m). **[933]** Population Institute, Washington, DC. **[934]** Central TV. Alzheimer's Disease is one of the afflictions 'revealed' by an ageing population. **[935]** World Fertility Survey, quoted in A. Rodda, *Women and the Environment.* **[936]** UNFPA, *State of the World Population 1990* (1986). **[937]** UNFPA *State of the World Population 1990* (1986). **[938]** *Catholic Herald.* **[939]** *Catholic Herald.* **[940]** WHO (1992). Another 9,000 die from diarrhoeal sickness and 10,000 from pneumonia. Until children survive, parents will have too many. **[941]** WHO (1992). Child mortality has been reduced by 120,000 per year over the last five years. The only way to persuade parents that their children will survive, and that they therefore do not need to have more than one or two, is to teach mothers hygiene, to eradicate disease, and to supply family planning. **[942]** WHO (1992). **[943]** RM/Population Institute, Washington, DC. Estimated total of 1.5bn. The rich world seems indifferent as millions die under age five, yet if poor people felt confident that their babies would survive, they would take measures (as along as they were available) to have fewer. The worldwide education of women in hygiene and literacy is the only answer. **[944]** Population Institute, Washington, DC. **[945]** Population Institute, Washington, DC. **[946]** Population Insight, UNFPA. **[947]** BBC TV, *Panorama*. **[948]** M. French, *The War Against Women*. **[949]** A. Milne, *Our Drowning World*. **[950]** A. Milne, *Our Drowning World*. **[951]** J. Gottman. Covering an area of 53,000 sq miles. **[952]** UNFPA. **[953]** UNFPA. **[954]** WHO (1992). **[955]** WHO (1992). **[956]** WHO (1992). **[957]** WHO (1992). **[958]** WHO (1992). Three-quarters of the preventable disease-related deaths occur in developing countries. **[959]** WHO (1992). **[960]** Philippe Frossard, *The Lottery of Life*. **[961]** Marie Stopes International. Every hour, 164,000,000, 60bn a year. **[962]** Marie Stopes International (1991 estimate). Every year, 250,000 with many more being rendered sterile or having their health ruined. **[963]** Marie Stopes International. About 330m women. A rate of 75 per cent is considered necessary to stabilise the world population at 10bn, or nearly twice the current total. **[964]** Marie Stopes International. A total of 1.218bn of them must be practising family planning to prevent world population passing 10bn towards the end of the 21st century, according to MSI. **[965]** Marie Stopes International (1991 estimate). **[966]** Marie Stopes International. Current developing world annual expenditure on family planning is about $3,200m, 20 per cent of it foreign aid, another 20 per cent user purchases, the rest from local governments. **[967]** Paul Harrison/WDM Experts Conference. A doubling of the current world population of 5,400m within a lifetime. **[968]** RM/Marie Stopes International. **[969]** James D. Watson. **[970]** UNFPA, *State of the World Population 1990* (1986). **[971]** WHO (1992). The high estimate is 40m. **[972]** BBC News. **[973]** WHO. **[974]** *National Geographic*. While everyone wishes to live a long life, it is quality, not quantity which counts. Helena Norberg-Hodge recounts in *Ancient Futures: Learning From Ladakh*, that Ladakhis, while not having a long life expectancy by US or European standards, nevertheless remain fit, enjoy life and work until they drop. By contrast, medical science is creating a 10- to 20-year degenerative limbo at the end of the life cycle. **[975]** WHO (1992). **[976]** WHO (1992). **[977]** WHO (1992). **[978]** WHO (1992). **[979]** WHO (1992). **[980]** *Quid* (1989). **[981]** *Quid* (1989). **[982]** *Quid* (1989). **[983]** World Fertility Survey, quoted in A. Rodda, *Women and the Environment*. **[984]** World Fertility Survey, quoted in A. Rodda, *Women and the Environment*. **[985]** Worldwatch Institute. **[986]** Euromonitor. **[987]** Colin Johnson, *Fourth World Review*. **[988]** Colin Johnson, *Fourth World Review*. **[989]** Euromonitor. **[990]** *Fourth World Review*. **[991]** UN Population Fund. Murray Bookchin, the ecologist who argues for putting the social programme first, criticises population campaigners Paul and Anne Ehrlich for making no distinction between the poor and their corporate predators, such as Europe's Nestlé's, which marketed baby milk-powder to poor countries, depriving infants of the vital disease-fighting ingredients of mothers' milk. Far from increasing population, healthy babies persuade parents that their line will survive with fewer heirs. **[992]** Euromonitor. *In Context* magazine notes that the nation with the lowest fertility rate (1.3 children per woman) is Italy, home of the Catholic Church. **[993]** RM/UNFPA. A total increase of 2.6bn. **[994]** A. Milne, *Our Drowning World*. It is hard to turn round a process driven by trillions of dollars of socially destructive development within a few years. While people feel their children may not survive, they will have too many. The solution to overpopulation lies in the education of women, the nurturing of the young, and the provision of family planning. **[995]** RM/ Population Institute, Washington, DC. An Indian woman's fertility is currently 4.7 births per woman. **[996]** RM/UNFPA. **[997]** UNFPA. A total of 50m. **[998]** World bank (1.6bn). **[999]** RM/UNFPA. A total of 17m. **[1000]** RM/Population Institute, Washington, DC. A total of 70m. **[1001]**RM/UNFPA. A total of 700m people. **[1002]** Population Concern. **[1003]** Population Concern. Reached in 1830. **[1004]** Population Concern. **[1005]** Population Concern. **[1006]** RM/Perdita Huston. **[1007]** Neils Skakkebaek, *The Independent on Sunday* (8 March 1992). **[1008]** *Nature* 346, 349 (1990/91). The BMA in *Hazardous Waste and Human Health* reports Swiss research that suggests the average human corpse emits up to one gram of mercury vapour and a smaller amount of lead vapour when it is cremated. A sample British crematorium carried out 3,831 cremations, giving the listed probable emission. The source is believed to be dental amalgam fillings. Lead vapour's source is unknown. Mercury is a high-danger pollutant. **[1009]** WHO (1992). The other 20 per cent are a crucial priority. **[1010]** Tony Worthington, MP. **[1011]** Tony Worthington, MP. **[1012]** UNFPA, *State of the World Population 1990* (1986). African girls' secondary school enrolment is 55 per cent that of boys. **[1013]** UNFPA, *State of the World Population 1990* (1986). More girls are enrolled than boys. **[1014]** UNFPA, *State of the World Population 1990* (1986). Arab girls' secondary-school enrolment is 70 per cent that of boys. **[1015]** UNFPA, *State of the World Population 1990* (1986). Asian girls' secondary-school enrolment is 70 per cent that of boys. **[1016]** A. Rodda, *Women and the Environment* (1985).

RESOURCE CONTROL [1017] J. Rifkin, *Beyond Beef*. The digestive tracts of these animals produce a huge amount of methane gas, one of the most problematic greenhouse-effect contributors. Beef-eating human populations have to learn to wean themselves off beef. Frances Moore Lappé's *Diet For A Small Planet* is the definitive book on the subject. **[1018]** World Resources Institute. **[1019]** R. North. **[1020]** R. North. **[1021]** R. North. **[1022]** R. North. **[1023]** R. North. **[1024]** R. North. **[1025]** *E, the Environmental Magazine* (May/June 1992). **[1026]** Euromonitor, *Consumer USA* (1990). The average American eats 19.8lbs of confectionery per year. **[1027]** R. North. **[1028]** R. North. **[1029]** RM/

Euromonitor, *Consumer USA* (1990). 2.8bn lbs. **[1030]** *The New International*ist. **[1031]** *The New Internationalist.* **[1032]** WDM Experts Conference (1990). Awareness is growing of debt's contribution to world pollution. **[1033]** Euromonitor, *Consumer USA* (1990). Total is $1.8bn at recommended price in 1990. More than half of all US adults use antacids. **[1034]** *The Ecologist.* In 1992 at an English farm shop outside London 10lbs of English new potatoes were being sold at 20 pence per lb, and 10lb of Egyptian new potatoes were being sold at 10 pence per lb – a hideous example of poor countries being forced to export their desperately needed food at ludicrously unreal prices. **[1035]** *The Ecologist.* Forty million tons. For a thorough attack on rich countries' indulgence in a beef-led diet, see *Beyond Beef*, by Jeremy Rifkin. **[1036]** J.N. Belden, *Dirt Rich, Dirt Poor.* Three million acres. **[1037]** R. Body. Estimated between 1975 and 1980. **[1038]** *The Ecologist.* In the UK, the average farm size is 170 acres. **[1039]** *Earth Report 2.* Total is 212,000 tons. **[1040]** *Earth Report 2.* Total is 4.2m tons. **[1041]** *The Ecologist.* Fifty million tons. **[1042]** *The Ecologist.* One hundred million tons. **[1043]** *The Ecologist.* **[1044]** RM/Rob Pardy (1978). Pro-rated at 5 per cent per annum from Pardy's 1978 estimate. **[1045]** Prof. D.N. Rao, Benares Hindu University. Prof. Rao's high estimate is 30 per cent. **[1046]** Carrying Capacity, Washington, DC. **[1047]** London Food Commission. Of the food additives 3,880 are cosmetic in purpose. **[1048]** *Farmers Weekly.* **[1049]** *E, the Environmental Magazine* (May/June 1992). The Vindicator plant at Mulberry, Florida, currently only irradiates strawberries with cobalt-60, but the target volume is 600m lbs of produce per year. Export produce will be particularly targeted, because of the artificially long life given by the radioactive treatment. **[1050]** US Food and Drug Administration. **[1051]** Estimated by B. Stokes, a former Worldwatch Institute researcher (556m tons). **[1052]** Euromonitor: *Consumer USA.* In 1989 24bn lbs. **[1053]** WDM Experts Conference. **[1054]** US National Research Council. **[1055]** P. Frossard. Or $500m. **[1056]** P. Frossard. Or $300m. **[1057]** P. Frossard. **[1058]** *The Ecologist.* **[1059]** *The Ecologist.* **[1060]** J. Rifkin, *Beyond Beef.* Cattle release 12 per cent of all methane released into the atmosphere. Methane is a potent greenhouse-effect gas. **[1061]** The US Animal Welfare Institute (1987). **[1062]** *The Ecologist.* **[1063]** US National Research Council. **[1064]** WHO (1992). A total of 1.4bn living in poorly nourished countries is seen as an improvement, because in the 1960s one-third of the world's population had inadequate nutrition. **[1065]** WHO (1992). **[1066]** Euromonitor: *Consumer USA.* In 1990 $8.3bn. **[1067]** R. North, *The Real Cost.* A total of 130m tons. **[1068]** R. North, *The Real Cost.* A total of 240m tons. **[1069]** RM/Euromonitor: *Consumer USA* and *Information Please Almanac.* A total of $1.8bn was spent on filling the baby bottle instead of giving suck. 4.2m babies were born. Some of them were breast-fed for at least a few months, so the actual amount spent per baby is even more. Why do so many American women refuse such a fundamental children's right to their babies: human milk? **[1070]** E. Goldsmith and N. Hildyard, *The Social and Environmental Effects of Large Dams* (1984). **[1071]** E. Goldsmith and N. Hildyard, *The Social and Environmental Effects of Large Dams* (1984). Production rises 5 to 8 times with sugar beet and legumes, as much as 10 times with fodder. But aquifers are being mined for water faster than their replacement rate. **[1072]** World Resources Institute. The estimated range is 5 to 20 calories. **[1073]** World Resources Institute. **[1074]** *Farmers Weekly.* **[1075]** *Farmers Weekly.* **[1076]** *The Ecologist.* The water is now being pumped out faster than the replacement rate. **[1077]** *The Ecologist.* The low estimate is 25 years. **[1078]** The Pesticides Trust. An estimate by pesticides-awareness campaigners. Per year the total is 300m kgs, half of it going on an export crop, cotton. **[1079]** WHO/UN Environment Working Party. **[1080]** WHO/UN Environment Working Party (est). **[1081]** London Food Commission (1984). **[1082]** US National Research Council. **[1083]** London Food Commission (1984). **[1084]** London Food Commission (1984). Agents that could possibly cause birth mutations. **[1085]** *The Ecologist.* The US National Academy of Sciences reports that no safety data are available on 37 per cent of some 600 active ingredients in common use in pesticides. **[1086]** London Food Commission (1984). Agents that could possibly cause allergy conditions. **[1087]** US Food and Drug Administration. **[1088]** London Food Commission. **[1089]** WHO (1991). Often the episodes involve pesticides which have been refused licences for use in the USA, and whose US makers try to recoup costs by selling abroad. Ironically, products treated with such pesticides are then imported back into the USA. **[1090]** Earthscan (1977). **[1091]** Dr Malcolm Potts. One hundred-thousandth of world expenditure on arms in 1990. **[1092]** World Resources Institute. **[1093]** *The Ecologist.* **[1094]** Euromonitor: *Consumer USA.* **[1095]** Euromonitor: *Consumer USA.* **[1096]** Antonio Ciancullo. **[1097]** *E, the Environmental Magazine* (May/June 1992). Thirty-five thousand people. **[1098]** *The Ecologist.* **[1099]** *In Context,* citing *Worldwatch Magazine* (Aug 1989). **[1100]** R. North. **[1101]** The Tea Council. Some 2.5m tons. **[1102]** The Tea Council (1990). A total of 1.1m tons. This export crop, however damaging to India's local food production, threatens even greater problems by being lost to synthetic teas being researched in Northern laboratories. **[1103]** R. North. **[1104]** National Environmental Engineering and Resources Institute, India. **[1105]** WHO (1992). **[1106]** RM/WHO (1992). **[1107]** T. Scudder, *The Careless Technology* (1976). **[1108]** E. Goldsmith and N. Hildyard, *The Social and Environmental Effects of Large Dams* (1984). **[1109]** Goldsmith and Hildyard, *The Social and Environmental Effects of Large Dams* (1984). **[1110]** *The Ecologist.* Compared with 2.3 per cent in the UK.

SUPPLY HOLD [1111] WCED *Our Common Future.* **[1112]** UN FAO, *Potential Population Supporting Capacities of Lands In The Developing World* (1984). **[1113]** US Dept of Agriculture, cited in F. M. Lappé, *Diet For A Small Planet.* Irrigating enough grain to produce a pound of grain-fed meat takes from 500 to 1,000 US gallons of water. More than half the USA's harvested acreage is used to feed livestock. **[1114]** Mustafa K. Tolba, *Saving Our Planet.* **[1115]** Mustafa K. Tolba, *Saving Our Planet.* **[1116]** World Bank, *World Development Report* (1988). **[1117]** World Bank, *World Development Report* (1988). Americans eat too much protein, which affects their health. **[1118]** *Harpers* (May 1991). Factory-fed cattle are producing huge surpluses of manure slurry, which pollutes waterways. **[1119]** P. Harrison, *The Greening of Africa* (1987). A total of 742m hectares. **[1120]** UNEP. A total of 11bn acres, or 35 per cent of land surface. **[1121]** World Resources Institute. **[1122]** *Marine Conservation News* (USA). This Indian sub-continent dolphin is predicted to become extinct within 20–50 years. It survives only in a reserve. **[1123]** CITES 1992. Down from about 2.5m in 1970. **[1124]** *Critical Trends in the Environment* (1992). **[1125]** *Critical Trends in the Environment* (1992). All the reservations are being dropped except six on whales, which the Convention on International Trade In Endangered Species, CITES, is trying to end. **[1126]** *Critical Trends in the Environment* (1992). By contrast, groups in the USA and Europe have memberships in the hundreds of thousands. **[1127]** Meadows, Meadows and Rander, *Beyond The Limits.* **[1128]** Meadows, Meadows and Rander, *Beyond The Limits.* **[1129]** Dr David Suzuki, *Inventing the Future.* Another 200 are endangered. **[1130]** Dr David Suzuki, *Inventing the Future.* Of the remaining 204, 106 are endangered. **[1131]** US General Accounting Office. There is concern in the US Food and Drug Administration about the safety for human consumption of some of the drugs used. **[1132]** P. Harrison, *The Greening of Africa* (1987). 'Women do 90 per cent of the work on African farms,' Robert Rodale. **[1133]** Global Tomorrow Coalition. **[1134]** *Imperiled Planet*, MIT Books. This figure is distorted by Australia's huge outback sheep ranches. **[1135]** *Imperiled Planet.* US usage seems lower than Japan's, but the figure is distorted by America's huge plains. **[1136]** *Imperiled Planet.* **[1137]** *Imperiled Planet.* **[1138]** Mustafa K. Tolba, *Saving Our Planet.* Original numbers are estimated to have been at least 100,000. **[1139]** US Fish and Wildlife Service. **[1140]** Worldwatch Institute, Washington, DC. **[1141]** Conagra. In 1991 the pay of the Chair/CEO was $2,463,000 (US Securities and Exchange Commission). Profits were $311m (*Fortune*). **[1142]** *The Sunday Times* (17 May 1992). **[1143]** Sara Lee Corporation. (1991 profits of $535m on turnover of $12.4bn were up 13.8 per cent.) **[1144]** *Critical Trends in the Environment* (1992). President George Bush stepped in to reduce the raw log exports. **[1145]** *Information Please Almanac* (1992). **[1146]** Capt. Paul Watson, Sea Shepherd Conservation Society. Capt. Watson made his estimate after ramming Japanese fishboats in the North Pacific in 1990 to defend the millions of dolphin destroyed by the gillnets. Over 600 such nets are used by Japan and South Korea, as far away as the Caribbean sea. Japan agreed to make the practice illegal by the end of 1992 (*Marine Conservation News*). **[1147]** *Critical Trends in the Environment* (1992). Greenpeace estimates that 6,400 dolphin were killed in the three-month summer season of 1990, along with 900,000 tuna, 3,000 sunfish, 4,000 shark and 30,000 billfish. **[1148]** The Global Tomorrow Coalition (USA). After rocketing growth, grain output per person has declined since 1984. Much of the planting may have been ecologically unwise. **[1149]** Mustafa K. Tolba, *Saving Our Planet*. Original numbers of the humpback whale are believed to have been at least 20,000. **[1150]** P. Harrison, *The Greening of Africa* (1987). Nearly 1bn Africans are on a diet too poor for an active working life. **[1151]** UN FAO: *Potential Population Supporting Capacities of Lands in the Developing World* (1984). **[1152]** El Hinnawi and Hashmai, *The State of the Environment*. **[1153]** WHO. A total of 1.3bn people. **[1154]** W.S. Arbuckle, *Ice Cream* (1986). Australians eat 20 quarts per capita, compared to 21.5 quarts (73m gallons to 83m) in the USA. **[1155]** RM/US National Wildlife Federation (1991). 12.2bn bd ft per year. This cut (only 20 per cent of the national harvest) is planned to be reduced to 10.8bn by 1955, with a halving of ecologically insane clearcutting. These reductions are a sign of some welcome public-spiritedness in the corporately-dominated US Forest Service, but how can the USA possibly call on poor countries to curb rainforest felling while such fervent destruction is still occurring on its own territory? **[1156]** Mustafa K. Tolba, *Saving Our Planet*. **[1157]** Mustafa K. Tolba, *Saving Our Planet*. Coastal mangrove swamps serve as natural barriers to flooding from storms. Farmers overlook this when they convert them to rice fields and fish ponds. **[1158]** RM/F. M. Lappé, *Diet For A Small Planet* (1979). Twenty-one million tons. **[1159]** F.M. Lappé, Diet for a Small Planet (1979). A total of 145m tons. **[1160]** US Dept of Agriculture, cited in *Harpers* (June 1991). **[1161]** US Dept of Agriculture, cited in *Harpers* (June 1991). The cow pays for higher productivity by living a third of its natural life. **[1162]** EPA/US National Wildlife Federation (1991). There are also 75 chemical spills per month. **[1163]** The Wilderness Society (1989). Old growth means such things as 'largesaw timber', which is greater than 21″ diameter at breast height [dbh], but no formal US inventory exists. According to Earth First!, much of the US North-west's remaining old growth is 'fragmented beyond usefulness as old-growth habitat'. Combined area believed left is 1.3m acres. **[1164]** Chesapeake Bay Foundation. **[1165]** Pimentel and Levitan, *Bioscience* (Vol. 36, No. 2). **[1166]** David Pimentel. Integrated pest management makes use of pests' natural enemies. **[1167]** RM/trade sources. A total of 1,449,000 tons (1989). Some of the pig iron is smelted with virgin hardwood from tropical forests. In Brazil, rainforest hardwoods are burned to smelt pig iron for European car production. **[1168]** Dr David Suzuki, *Inventing the Future*. Only about 150 have been grown commercially, and 'human nutrition today is based on only 20 or so major crops!' **[1169]** Dr David Suzuki, *Inventing the Future*. **[1170]** *The Ecologist*. Forty million cu m. **[1171]** SustainAbility. **[1172]** *The Ecologist*. **[1173]** Dr David Suzuki, *Inventing the Future*. Six million hectares, leaving only 2m hectares. Only 2.2 per cent of Australia is forest. **[1174]** RM/World Resources Institute. **[1175]** *National Geographic*. *In Context* magazine notes that forest in the former Soviet Union is being destroyed as fast as it is in Brazil. **[1176]** *National Geographic*. **[1177]** Geo. **[1178]** RM/*Alternatives* (Vol. 18, No. 1, 1991). Twenty million cu metres. **[1179]** CITES 1992. Bear paws and gallbladders are also valued for medicinal and aphrodisiac use, and the Asian bear has been virtually wiped out, while the USA allows the traffic in bear parts. **[1180]** World Resources Institute. The shellfish would make a 141-mile tailback of nose-to-tail semi-trailer trucks. **[1181]** US Dept of Commerce: National Oceanic & Atmospheric Administration. **[1182]** Paul Ehrlich. Smithsonian Institute biologist Terry Erwin, conducting a hurried inventory of vanishing rainforests, considers that his 30m estimate could well be proved conservative. He has found as many as 10,000 species in one tree, many of them unknown. **[1183]** World Resources Institute. **[1184]** World Resources Institute. This figure, until recently considered a high one, is now becoming discredited. **[1185]** Terry Erwin, Smithsonian Institute, Washington, DC. **[1186]** World Resources Institute (1991). Estimates of world species numbers range from a minimum of 30m (Terry Erwin, Smithsonian Institute) to 80m (Paul Ehrlich). **[1187]** Mustafa K. Tolba, *Saving Our Planet*. Citing the International Whaling Commission's 1989 estimate. **[1188]** Mustafa K. Tolba, *Saving Our Planet*. Citing the International Whaling Commission's 1989 estimate. **[1189]** *The Earth First! Reader* (1991). **[1190]** Dr David Suzuki, *Inventing the Future*. Suzuki lists BC's neighbour, Alberta, saving 9.1 per cent; US logging states Washington and Idaho protecting 11.3 and 9.7 per cent; California 10 per cent; Alaska nearly 40 per cent; Tanzania 25 per cent; and New Zealand 17.1 per cent. Fortunately, a progressive government was elected in BC in 1991 with more far-sighted policies. On current performance, all BC's formerly vast areas of wilderness will have vanished. **[1191]** Mustafa K. Tolba, *Saving Our Planet*. A total of 960m cubic metres; 2,400m people rely on wood for domestic heating and cooking. In his book *Earthrise*, Herbert Girardet describes flying over Khartoum, capital of the Sudan, and seeing the vast 120-mile radius circle round the city where people too poor to buy gas or kerosene have used their donkeys or camels to clear the trees. He reports that Nairobi is similarly denuded. **[1192]** World Resources Institute. Forty million acres a year, or an area equivalent to the US state of Washington, is cut and cleared. **[1193]** *Critical Trends in the Environment* (1992). **[1194]** RM. A total of 13.5m cu metres. **[1195]** RM. A total of 27.7m cu metres. **[1196]**

CITES 1992. In spite of the critical damage to bluefin tuna numbers, the USA, Canada, Japan and Morocco refused Sweden's call for a total ban, only agreeing to cut their catches by 50 per cent. **[1197]** *Critical Trends in the Environment* (1992). **[1198]** *Critical Trends in the Environment* (1992). CITES imposed a ban for the end of 1992. Critics claimed Japan had built up a stockpile of 18,000 carcasses in 1991. The turtle has lived on earth for 150m years. **[1199]** *Critical Trends in the Environment* (1992). Shell from endangered hawksbill turtles is made into jewellery, combs, etc. Hundreds of miles of their egg-laying beaches in Eastern Florida are built up, and patrolled by egg-crushing police and other vehicles. Egg-rescuing efforts are patchy. Japan aimed to import 7,500kg of hawksbill shell between mid-1991 and the end of 1992, representing nearly 7,500 turtles (US Dept of Fish & Wildlife). In early 1992 Japanese officials said their country would become a world environmental leader. **[1200]** World Resources Institute. **[1201]** World Resources Institute. **[1202]** International Joint Commission. **[1203]** *Time* (20 Aug 1990). **[1204]** RM/*Time* (20 Aug 1990). **[1205]** World Resources Institute. The Ogallala aquifer underlies 170,000 square miles of the North American Great Plains, formed during the Ice Ages. (Compare with entry 1077 for speculative nature of human water resources.) **[1206]** Environment Canada. **[1207]** Environment Canada. **[1208]** Environment Canada. **[1209]** RM/World Resources Institute. About 100,000 US gallons of water go into the production of one new car. **[1210]** World Resources Institute. **[1211]** RM/World Resources Institute. A total of 30.8bn gallons. **[1212]** Settlement Watch, Washington, DC, cited in *Harpers* (May 1992). **[1213]** J. Robbins, *Diet For A New America*. **[1214]** H. Patricia *Earthright* and *Every Citizen's Guide*. **[1215]** Global Tomorrow Coalition (USA). **[1216]** World Resources Institute. **[1217]** J. Robbins, *Diet For A New America*. **[1218]** Georgia Pacific Corporation. **[1219]** Zaïre Tropical Forest Action Plan. **[1220]** Zaïre Tropical Forest Action Plan.

ON BOARD ENERGY SYSTEMS [1221] *Flight International*. Average daily gasoline consumption of each American is 4,604 litres (total 1990 shipments 111bn US gallons). One hundred and ten passengers emptying the tank of an MD-11 use up 1,380 litres each, or 300 times average daily gasoline use of Americans per capita. In a compact car, 1,380 litres would take an American driver about 11,000 miles (at 30 m.p.USg.), or a generous year's driving ration. That's a YEAR'S driving ration in one short flight! **[1222]** Argonne National Laboratory. **[1223]** Argonne National Laboratory. **[1224]** Argonne National Laboratory. **[1225]** Argonne National Laboratory. **[1226]** Worldwatch Institute. Far exceeding car production of 44m (1987). **[1227]** Worldwatch Institute. **[1228]** Meadows, Meadows and Randers, *Beyond The Limits*. The authors point out that a car comes from the earth and returns there. 'If an eventual 12.5bn people all consumed materials at the rate of the average late-20th-century

American, that would require an increase in worldwide steel production by a factor of 7, copper by a factor of 11, and aluminium by a factor of 12.' **[1229]** Mustafa K. Tolba, *Saving Our Planet*. 'About half were constructed in China alone.' Tolba notes that water stored in man-made reservoirs almost equals the total worldwide annual water withdrawal. **[1230]** *Wall Street Journal*, cited in Echeverric, Burrow and Roos-Collins, *Rivers At Risk*. One for every 3,187 US residents. The US National Park Service has put the figure at 75,000, the EPA at least 68,000. Hydro power in the US went from 96m MWh in 1950 to 280m MWh in 1990. **[1231]** *The Guardian* (6 April 1992). **[1232]** T.W. Mermel (1991). **[1233]** T.W. Mermel (1991). **[1234]** *The Ecologist*. **[1235]** *The State of India's Environment* (1982). **[1236]** *The State of India's Environment* (1982). **[1237]** *Nuclear Engineering International* (1991). **[1238]** *Nuclear Engineering International* (1991). **[1239]** *Nuclear Engineering International* (1991). **[1240]** OECD. **[1241]** OECD. **[1242]** OECD. **[1243]** *Critical Trends in the Environment* (1992). **[1244]** Rocky Mountain Institute, cited by *Critical Trends in the Environment*, (1992). **[1245]** EPA, *Green Lights* (1992). **[1246]** *Critical Trends in the Environment* (1992). **[1247]** *Critical Trends in the Environment*, (1992). **[1248]** *Critical Trends in the Environment*, (1992). **[1249]** Union of Concerned Scientists, *Steering a New Course*. Current pump cost is about $1.20. Social costs include hidden overheads such as environmental, health and other problems resulting from energy production and consumption. **[1250]** RM/World Resources Institute (1990). Up to 50 per cent of it imported. **[1251]** RM/World Resources Institute (1990). **[1252]** RM/World Resources Institute (1990). **[1253]** Meadows, Meadows and Randers, *Beyond The Limits*. The authors point out that depletion of oil plus combustion problems of coal could throw dependence on to gas. Without new discoveries, we are set to burn out gas at 5 per cent annual growth by 2040. **[1254]** World Resources Institute/*Information Please Environmental Almanac* (1992). This increase came in spite of fuel conservation, because sheer human numbers increased. It is the USA which is the most seriously overpopulated country in the world. **[1255]** Texaco Inc. The corporation's 1991 profits were $1.3bn. **[1256]** World Resources Institute (1988). **[1257]** World Resources Institute (1988). **[1258]** LINK Resources Corp. **[1259]** LINK Resources Corp. **[1260]** RM/World Resources Institute (1990). **[1261]** Federal Energy Regulatory Commission. **[1262]** US EPA. **[1263]** RM/World Resources Institute (1990). **[1264]** Michael Renner, Worldwatch Institute. **[1265]** RM/David Levine. **[1266]** Nuclear Electric plc. The meltdown at Chernobyl in the Ukraine on 24 April 1986 showed that thousands of square miles could be irradiated by a meltdown. About 6m people live in a horseshoe of five nuclear-power stations in England's north-west. There is no provision of precautionary iodine tablet supplies to the public in the region, and tablet supplies at the plants appear derisory. **[1267]** Guy Dauncey, *After the Crash*. **[1268]** *Nuclear Engineer-*

ing International (1991). **[1269]** *Nuclear Engineering International* (1991). **[1270]** *Nuclear Engineering International* (1990). 13,993 MWe total. The UK's new Sizewell nuclear plant would need to be built 60 times to match Japan's reactor programme to the year 2010 (SustainAbility). **[1271]** *Nuclear Engineering International* (1991). **[1272]** RM/Uranium Producers of America. **[1273]** *The Ecologist*. **[1274]** RM/Atomic Energy Control Board of Canada (1984). Ten million tons a year. **[1275]** RM/Rosalie Bertelle. **[1276]** International Physicians for the Prevention of Nuclear War. Not forgetting the 106 also carried out by the USA in Pacific areas. **[1277]** International Physicians for the Prevention of Nuclear War. **[1278]** International Physicians for the Prevention of Nuclear War. **[1279]** International Physicians for the Prevention of Nuclear War. **[1280]** International Physicians for the Prevention of Nuclear War. And a further 90 tests in Novaya Zamla. **[1281]** International Physicians for the Prevention of Nuclear War. And another nine at Christmas Island, Polynesia. **[1282]** International Physicians for the Prevention of Nuclear War. **[1283]** International Atomic Energy Agency. Most of the nuclear waste was dumped in the North-East Atlantic. **[1284]** UK Dept of Transport (1990). **[1285]** RM/World Resources Institute (1990). **[1286]** RM/World Resources Institute (1990). **[1287]** D. Brown, *Who Killed Alaska?* UNCED quotes 40,878 cu metres. If anything is more disturbing than the Exxon Valdez catastrophe and California's continuing increase in fuel consumption following it, it is the report in *Harpers* (March 1991) that only eight per cent of the Exxon Valdez oil has been removed from the spill environment. **[1288]** World Resources Institute. A total of 2,500,000 bbls. **[1289]** UK Dept of the Environment (1989). The equivalent of 557 heavy articulated truckloads. **[1290]** Exxon Corporation. In 1991 profits were $5.6bn, up 11.8 per cent. Sidney Reso, boss of Exxon's international division, was kidnapped in 1992, after the company's cost-cutting led to a rash of oil-spills, with no double-hulled tankers in the fleet. Nine oil-spill experts left the company 1985–92. A whistle-blower claims there was bribery over the Exxon Valdez Alaskan spill clean-up. Exxon strip-purchases downwind from plants and destroys homes to evade eco-regulations, and flirts with 'wise-use' fanatics eager to drill in Alaska wildlife refuges. **[1291]** SustainAbility. A $1bn petrochemical plant is under construction at Port Harcourt, while British financial authorities are warning that corruption and deception are a way of life in Nigeria. **[1292]** *Environment* (March 1992). **[1293]** Elsworth, *A Dictionary Of The Environment*. **[1294]** RM/SustainAbility. A total of 1.4m hectares, down from 2.1m a decade earlier. **[1295]** Echeverric, Burrow and Roos-Collins, *Rivers At Risk*. **[1296]** Echeverric, Burrow and Roos-Collins, *Rivers At Risk*. **[1297]** International Physicians for the Prevention of Nuclear War. **[1298]** *The Ecologist*. **[1299]** RM/*Statistical Abstract of the US* (1985–90). The world tanker fleet is aging. Many vessels are obsolete, their owners changing flags to seek laxer regulations, the replacement cost of vessels being prohibitive. **[1300]** LINK

Resources Corp. **[1301]** International Physicians for the Prevention of Nuclear War. **[1302]** RM/Motor Vehicle Manufacturers' Association of America (1989: 556,931,000 extrapolated at three per cent per annum). **[1303]** RM/*World Population Data Sheet* and *The Economist*. US registered cars, trucks and buses (210m, pro rata at four per cent from 187m in 1989) use some 111bn US gallons of gasoline per year. World consumption at US vehicle penetration would be in the region of 1.6trn US gallons per year, or 4.4bn US gallons a day, or 1.2m gallons a minute. **[1304]** RM/ World Resources Institute/*1992 Information Please Environmental Almanac*. **[1305]** Worldwatch Institute. **[1306]** Worldwatch Institute. **[1307]** Center for Economic Conversion. **[1308]** *The Ecologist*. Causing 4,000 additional lung-cancer deaths from radon gas in local communities. **[1309]** RM/*The Ecologist*. A total of 82,000 miles, loaded with 191m tons of tailings. **[1310]** World Resources Institute. Low estimate is seven US gallons. **[1311]** RM/World Resources Institute (1990). Horizontal drilling produces more than twice as much. **[1312]** RM/World Resources Institute (1990). **[1313]** Nuclear Engineering International (1991). General Electric have built 62, Skoda 20, Toshiba 11 and Hitachi 8.

CLIMATE CONTROL [1314] Worldwatch Institute. **[1315]** John Seymour, *Changing Lifestyles*. **[1315a]** *The Lancet*. **[1316]** *Chicago Tribune* (8 May 1990). **[1317]** *Nature*. **[1318]** *Nature*. **[1319]** *Nature*, (4 July 1990). **[1320]** Worldwatch Institute (1985). China currently has only 1.2m cars, but Hong Kong entrepreneurs are aggressively opening driving schools in South China as Japanese and Korean car makers open vehicle plants. Soon the hush of cycle wheels on the streets of south China's towns and cities will be a forgotten memory and the world will have a new frontier of environmental crisis. **[1321]** Worldwatch Institute (1985). India has only 1.5m cars, or 30 bikes to every car. **[1322]** Worldwatch Institute (1985). But the USA has 139m cars, so only 0.7 bikes to cars. Because the USA has built a car-dependent environment, bicycles are used for recreation on, for example, reclaimed railroad routes. **[1323]** *State of the World 1990*. Worldwatch Institute (1986). **[1324]** *State of the World 1990* (1986). **[1325]** *State of the World 1990* (1986). Much of the Netherlands' network of cycle routes is direct and uninterrupted, for real journeying, not recreation or partial traffic relief. **[1326]** *National Geographic* (Vol. 177, No. 2). **[1327]** *National Geographic* (Vol. 177, No. 2). **[1328]** Antonio Ciancullo, *La Repubblica*. An estimated 2bn tons (1988). **[1329]** Antonio Ciancullo, *La Repubblica*. A total of 5.6bn tons. **[1330]** *1992 Information Please Environmental Almanac*. **[1331]** *UNCED/The Rio Treaties*, Adamantine Books (1992). Authoritative scientific forums in the years preceding the summit had agreed that 60 per cent cuts were required immediately to prevent climate interference. **[1332]** Worldwatch Institute. The reduction is attributed to economic recession in coal-burning former Soviet Union and Eastern Europe. The reduction is microscopic compared to the 5.5bn ton total. **[1333]** *The Ecologist*. Denmark increased its traffic speed limit to 110 kph from 100 kph in 1992, adding to its carbon dioxide emissions in direct opposition to the required trend. **[1334]** H. Patricia Hynes, *Earthright*. This is a 'ballpark' figure. **[1335]** US National Academy of Sciences. **[1336]** Antonio Ciancullo, *La Repubblica* and British Nuclear Fuels plc. **[1337]** Antonio Ciancullo, *La Repubblica*. **[1338]** Mustafa K. Tolba, *Saving Our Planet*. **[1339]** US Congress, Office of Technology Assessment, *Changing By Degrees*. **[1340]** US Congress, Office of Technology Assessment, *Changing By Degrees*. **[1341]** UNCED 1992, *USA National Report*. Reduction? No! The USA had even less of the world's population – five per cent. **[1342]** US Congress, Office of Technology Assessment, *Changing By Degrees*. **[1343]** *Environmental Effects of Ozone Depletion: 1991 Update*. UNEP. **[1344]** *Statistical Abstract of the USA* (1988/89). Days the city failed to meet ambient air quality standards. **[1345]** *Statistical Abstract of the USA* (1989). Up from 12.3 the year before – there's nothing like growth! All you need is a sense of tumour. **[1346]** Aubrey Meyer and UN Data (1988). **[1347]** Aubrey Meyer and UN Data (1988). **[1348]** *Wall Street Journal* (20 April 1990). **[1349]** *Automotive News, USA*. Champion dealer of 1991! Well done, Ed! And you can bet they were all CFC air-conditioned! **[1350]** RM/*Planet Drum*. **[1351]** *Times 1000* (1990). Net profits of £1,257m on a turnover of £12,906m ($21,940m). When NASA revealed urgently in early 1992 that Europe's ozone layer was badly damaged, ICI hurriedly announced that it was bringing forward its CFC phase-out date. Welcome news, perhaps, but why was ICI still making supertanker loads of CFCs when the scientific world had known of the risks since 1974? **[1352]** UNCED 92, *USA National Report*. El Dupont De Nemours Corp. makes a quarter of the world's CFCs. Its investment in alternatives promises to be recouped by US taxpayer subsidies of their purchase by developing countries. **[1353]** *Fortune* (1991). Dupont's profits were down 39 per cent from 1990, but still exceeded by 40 per cent the investment the company proposed to make in researching CFC alternatives over the next few years. The Chair/CEO pays himself $1,338,928 a year, or $5,149 per shift for being clever enough to make a major contribution to ruining the planet we inhabit, ignoring warnings which were first made in 1974. **[1354]** *Worldwatch Paper 87*. A total of 238,000 tons. CFC-11 lasts 76 years in the upper atmosphere. **[1355]** H. Patricia Hynes, *Earthright*. AT&T says the use of CFC-113 is to be phased out by the end of 1994. The only thing is, the dangers of CFCs were spelled out by scientists in 1974. That makes 18 years that corporations like AT&T have knowingly been risking wrecking Planet Earth for profit. **[1356]** *Worldwatch Paper 87*. A total of 138,000 tons. CFC-113 had the fastest-growing usage before the ozone-layer crisis, and lasts 92 years in the upper atmosphere. **[1357]** *Worldwatch Paper 87*. A total of 412,000 tons. About 40 per cent of CFC-12 is still in the upper atmosphere in 139 years' time. It has up to 10,000 times the heat retaining power of carbon dioxide, a fact complicated by UNEP's finding that reduced upper-atmospheric ozone might be having a cooling effect. **[1358]** RM/Allied Signal Inc. Why has Allied Signal been ignoring warnings of CFC dangers first published in 1974? The corporation's turnover in 1991 was $11.9bn. **[1359]** UNCED 92, *USA National Report*. **[1360]** *New York Times*. California scientists first warned the world of CFCs' deadly danger to the upper atmosphere in 1974. Although the USA acted fast to outlaw CFC-powered aerosols, industrial, computer, appliance and automotive use of the planet-murdering gases remains alarmingly enormous. **[1361]** *Statistical Record of the Environment*. Each A/C unit uses 2.5lbs of CFCs, plus 1lb for annual recharge. **[1362]** H. Patricia Hynes, *Earthright*. Two million lbs. **[1363]** H. Patricia Hynes, *Earthright*. **[1364]** Robert Mugabe (8 May 1992). **[1365]** Heinemann Philip. **[1366]** Heinemann Philip. **[1367]** Catherine Caulfield, *In the Rainforest* (1985), cited in Alex Shonmatoff, *Murder in the Rain Forest*, 1992, p. 270. **[1368]** Alex Shonmatoff, *Murder in the Rain Forest*, 1992, p. 270. **[1369]** US Dept of Commerce. At this rate, a car pumps out its own weight in carbon dioxide in a year, on average mileage. The US Corporate Average Fuel Economy (CAFE), currently 27.5 mpg, should be raised to 45 mpg by the year 2000, according to 80 per cent of respondents in a major 1990 survey of public opinion. **[1370]** H. Patricia Hynes, *Earthright*. This Volvo gets 63 mpg in the city, 81 on the highway. There are calls for an enforced US mpg rate (CAFE) of 48 mpg by 2000 (from 19.5 to 33 mpg for trucks). **[1371]** *Wall Street Journal* (20 April 1990). **[1372]** International Panel on Climate Change. By 2100, 4C if major cutbacks of about 60 per cent on current emissions are not achieved. **[1373]** UNCED 1992, *USA National Report*. **[1374]** Aubrey Meyer. **[1375]** *Facts on File*. Roger Revelle directed the Scripps Institute of Oceanography, California, USA, for years. He was born in 1909. **[1376]** H. Patricia Hynes, *Earthright*. **[1377]** *Automotive News, USA*. **[1378]** *Automotive News, USA*. **[1379]** Mustafa K. Tolba, *Saving Our Planet*. **[1380]** Mustafa K. Tolba, *Saving Our Planet*. **[1381]** *Facts on File* (4 January 1991). **[1382]** *Nature*. **[1383]** Worldwatch Institute. **[1384]** Worldwatch Institute. Poland's emissions are proportionally higher, but the planet doesn't care. **[1385]** *The Economist*. **[1386]** *Planet Drum*. **[1387]** Alan Gottlieb, ed., *The Wise Use Agenda*. **[1388]** Mustafa K. Tolba, *Saving Our Planet*. NASA now reports statistically meaningful ozone depletions of three to five per cent north of latitude 35 degrees north in springtime, and depletion as great as nine per cent at 45 degree north in winter, indicating a possible 900,000 blindings in the future. **[1389]** *Worldwatch Paper 87*. A total of 66,000 tons. It lasts 67 years in the upper atmosphere and is used mostly for solvents in, for example, electronics. **[1390]** Worldwatch Institute. Twenty supertanker cargoes. Upper atmospheric chlorine levels are set to triple by 2075, levels of much more aggressive bromine than before. **[1391]** H. Patricia Hynes, *Earthright*. **[1392]** *Worldwatch Paper 87*. A total of 6,000 tons. Halon 1301 lasts 101 years and halon 1211, 12 years in the upper atmosphere. Used in fire extinguishers, and a fast-growing product. **[1393]** *Worldwatch Paper 87*. A total of 474,000 tons. It lasts eight years in the upper atmosphere, and is used mostly in solvents in, for example, electronics. **[1394]** H. Patricia Hynes, *Earthright*. **[1395]** H. Patricia Hynes, *Earthright*. **[1396]** H. Patricia Hynes, *Earthright*. **[1397]** Mustafa K. Tolba, *Saving Our Planet*. Decreased from about 65m tons to 40m tons. **[1398]** Mustafa K. Tolba, *Saving Our Planet*. Increased from about 48m to 59m tons. **[1399]** Mustafa K. Tolba, *Saving Our Planet*. The conclusion of UNEP Global Environment Monitoring System (GEMS/AIR). One billion people are exposed to excessive levels of particulates. The vast majority consist of the working masses, showing that the old struggle for class justice and the struggle for a clean environment are now one and the same. **[1400]** Italian Tourist Office. Florence is a pedestrian mall during the day, and Strasbourg recently followed suit. **[1401]** *Statistical Record of the Environment* (1989). **[1402]** Global Releaf. **[1402a]** *Life* magazine. **[1403]** Prime Minister Bob Hawke (20 July 1989). **[1404]** *Life* magazine. **[1405]** US Wilderness Society. A total of 3.1m acres. **[1406]** Wanagri Mathai. It is now widely recognised that the key to saving the planet lies in educating women. Wanagri Mathai should be put in charge of that programme, not put in Kenyan jails. **[1407]** *Critical Trends in the Environment*. **[1408]** *Automotive News, USA* and *1991 Market Data Book*. Sixteen out of 1,170 photographed in *Automotive News*. **[1409]** *Automotive News, USA*. **[1410]** *Automotive News, USA*. **[1411]** *Automotive News, USA*. **[1412]** *Automotive News, USA*. **[1413]** *Automotive News, USA*. **[1414]** *Automotive News, USA*. **[1415]** Jeremy Rifkin, *Biosphere Politics*.

WASTE MANAGEMENT **[1416]** *Resource Recycling* (May/June 1989). (435,000 tons in 1988, up by 28 per cent.) Aluminium recycling is a source of super-deadly dioxins, the world's most potent poisons. **[1417]** BioCycle (1992). **[1418]** BioCycle (1992). The programme aims to pick up and dismantle safely 40/45,000 fridges per year. **[1419]** US Environmental Protection Agency 1990 (1988). **[1420]** SustainAbility. One-fifth of the energy is lost through inefficiency, or 2,000 supertanker loads. **[1421]** BioCycle (1991). Urgent studies are needed of the volume of wood and other valuable materials being dumped every day in construction waste. **[1422]** SustainAbility. **[1423]** SustainAbility (1991). **[1424]** RM/*The Official Steamship Guide* and *Statistical Record of the Environment*. Based on 16,427 cruising days in 1992/3 season with average 2,343 humans on board, generating typical 3lbs of waste per day, with 50 per cent being separated or incinerated on all ships, although only the most up-to-date follow such practices. Britain's QEII was photographed in 1990 dumping trash in the Caribbean. About a ton of trash per mile is retrieved from Texas's Caribbean beaches on pick-up days. The same goes for Venezuela's Caribbean shores. **[1425]** Procter & Gamble. Fiscal 1991 profits up 10 per cent on turnover of $27.4bn. Besides pollutant household cleaner products, the giant combine makes ecologically undesirable packaged foods, wasteful cellulose pulp and expensive patented pharmaceuticals. **[1426]** *Critical Trends in the Environment* (1992). **[1427]** SustainAbility. Stacks of rules and regulations may be necessary transitionally, but Kirkpatrick Sale argues in his book *Human Scale* (1980) that environmental law becomes superfluous when people control their own neighbourhoods using collective common sense. **[1428]** *Friends of the Earth* and *UK Dept of Energy Survey* (1985, revealed 1991). **[1429]** Chris Rose, *The Dirty Man of Europe*. **[1430]** BioCycle (1992). **[1431]** RM/ World Resources Institute. A total of 250m tons. The Environmental Protection Agency's estimate is lower, at 180m tons or just three times round the globe in semi-trailer trucks. The volume is rising, perhaps by 10 per cent by 2000. The US EPA plans to incinerate 20 per cent of it, recycle 25 per cent and landfill 55 per cent. Voices are being raised: why not reduce the volume instead? Impose charges on all packaging now, enforce reusable containers, boost waste disposal costs. **[1432]** Earth-Wise Inc, NY. **[1433]** *The State of India's Environment* (1982). Includes ½m litres of DDT. **[1434]** *Warmer Bulletin* (August 1991). **[1435]** Mustafa K. Tolba, *Saving Our Planet*. An estimated 6.5m tons. 'In one study, up to 70 per cent of the debris examined along the beaches of the Mediterranean was plastic; in the Pacific, the figure reached more than 80 per cent.' **[1436]** US Center for Marine Conservation, Washington, DC. A total of 129,000 volunteers on 4,085 miles of beach. Averaging 815lbs of waste per mile or nearly half a pound a yard. **[1437]** *Marine Conservation News* (US). A total of 1,500 volunteers on 21 Sept 1991. **[1438]** *Marine Conservation News* (US). A total of 450 volunteers. **[1439]** H. Patricia Hynes, *Earthright*. **[1440]** BioCycle (1992). **[1441]** BioCycle (1992). **[1442]** Earth-Wise Inc, NY. **[1443]** A Milne, *Our Drowning World*. **[1444]** *Critical Trends in the Environment* (1992). And well they might! No satisfactory method of dealing with waste from nuclear power plants (nuclear medical waste is peanuts compared) has yet been discovered. Originally driven by 1940s war madness, the industry jumped out of a plane and started trying to invent the parachute as it fell. The US government, like others, has spent mind-boggling amounts trying to build waste disposal facilities, without success. Now it has targeted poor Indians in remotest New Mexico. The waste must not leak for 10,000 years. **[1445]** *Critical Trends in the Environment* (1992). **[1446]** *Critical Trends in the Environment* (1992). **[1447]** H. Patricia Hynes, *Earthright*. **[1448]** Mustafa K. Tolba, *Saving Our Planet*. An estimate by the US National Research Council (3.2m tons) in 1985. Nearly half the amount is 'municipal wastes and run-off'. Shipping is now believed to account for some 568,800 tons of dumped oil per year, 20 per cent of it from spills. A less well-known phenomenon of environmental disruption is the countless millions of tons of sea-waters transported all over the world as ballast, then dumped, along with their loads of alien sea-life. **[1449]** BioCycle (1992). **[1450]** International Paper Corp. Fiscal 1991 turnover: $12.7bn or $48,846,153 a day. **[1451]** RM/World Resources Institute. **[1452]** EPA 1990 (1988). **[1453]** BioCycle (1992). This represents 60 per cent of the USA's sold waste paper tonnage. 2.2m tons go to Korea and Taiwan. **[1454]** Resource Recycling/American Paper Institute. Up 27.5 per cent, from 4.4m to 5.6m tons. **[1455]** Pulp & Paper (1992 estimate). From 20m tons to 25m. **[1456]** RM/Weyerhauser Co. Fiscal 1991 turnover $8.7bn. **[1457]** EPA. **[1458]** EPA. **[1459]** EPA 1990 (1988). **[1460]** RM/Franklin Associates Ltd. **[1461]** *Resource Recycling* (Oct 1990). A total of 130,600 tons, rising by 13 per cent a year. **[1462]** H. Patricia Hynes, *Earthright*. **[1463]** *Statistical Abstract of the US* 1991 (1988). A total of 200,000 tons are recycled, but 14.4m are dumped. **[1464]** EPA. **[1465]** EPA. **[1466]** RM/Franklin Associates Ltd. Americans discard some 1.5m PET bottles an hour. **[1467]** RM/Franklin Associates Ltd. **[1468]** RM/Franklin Associates Ltd. **[1469]** US National Propane Gas Association. Propane prolongs the life of engines, thereby reducing waste. **[1470]** *Statistical Record of the Environment*. A total of 40,752 cu m in 1988. **[1471]** H. Patricia Hynes, *Earthright*. **[1472]** Earth-Wise Inc, NY. **[1473]** *Garbage* (March/April 1991). **[1474]** SustainAbility. **[1475]** World Resources Institute. Many of the rivers are polluted by tin mines. The Prime Minister of Malaysia is reported as saying he wishes to increase his country's human population by four times. UK government arms salesmen consider Malaysia an important future client. **[1476]** RM/ *Resource Recycling*. Ten million tons in 1988. **[1477]** *Statistical Abstract of the USA* 1991 (1988). Only 700,000 tons are recovered from 11.6m tons. This may surprise people who believed scrapiron to be a long-standing model for the rest of the recycling industry. Steel recycling plants are major potential generators of super-deadly dioxins, the world's most potent poisons. **[1478]** UNCED. **[1479]** World Resources Institute. Only eight have complete treatment. **[1480]** *Chemical Engineering* (June 1991), cited in *Statistical Record of the Environment* (USA). **[1481]** EPA (1990). **[1481a]** EPA (1990). **[1482]** RM/*Statistical Abstract of the USA*. A total of 41,000 cu ft. **[1483]** RM/*Garbage* (Jan/Feb 1990). A total of 4.8bn gallons per day. The volume could easily be reduced about 70 per cent by low flush cisterns. **[1484]** RM/*Statistical Abstract of the USA*. There are 1,173 'superfund' waste sites (currently scheduled for hugely expensive clean-up) and some 31,000 others. **[1485]** EPA. A total of 1,621,231 short tons in 1988. **[1486]** Michael Levine, *The Environmental Address Book*. **[1487]** H. Patricia Hynes, *Earthright*. **[1488]** *The State of India's Environment* (1982). **[1489]** Goodyear Tire & Rubber. Fiscal 1991 turnover: $11bn. Plans are now afoot to incinerate a proportion of North America's junk tyres. If the US is incinerating a quarter of its garbage as well – how much incinerating can the atmosphere take? Would it not make more sense to retool and reduce motor vehicle use? **[1490]** Mustafa K. Tolba, *Saving Our Planet*. A further 73.5m bombs, shells and grenades have been recovered. **[1491]** Mustafa K. Tolba, *Saving Our Planet*. Tens of millions of other high-explosive munitions were also left unexploded. **[1492]** Mustafa K. Tolba, *Saving Our Planet*. About $850bn per year. Nearly all this amount will have to be switched to a global 'Marshall Plan' to save the world environment, as advocated by US Senator Al Gore in his landmark book *Earth In The Balance: Forging a New Common Purpose*. **[1493]** RM/Franklin Associates Ltd. **[1494]** RM/ Franklin Associates Ltd. **[1495]** EPA 1990 (1988). **[1496]** EPA (1991). **[1497]** EPA (1990). **[1498]** US National Solid Wastes Management Association. **[1499]** *Critical Trends in the Environment* (1992). **[1500]** *Critical Trends in the Environment* (1992). **[1501]** EPA. **[1502]** US National Solid Wastes Management Association. **[1503]** EPA. **[1504]** RM/ Michael Levine, *The Environmental Address Book*. **[1505]** Michael Levine, *The Environmental Address Book*.

Your suggestions for entries to this book are welcomed. Please write to Fourth Estate, marking the envelope *Planet Gauge*.